**Transforming Technology
Complete Self-Assessment Gui**

The guidance in this Self-Assessment is ....ısforming
Technology best practices and standards in business process
architecture, design and quality management. The guidance is also based
on the professional judgment of the individual collaborators listed in the
Acknowledgments.

Notice of rights

**You are licensed to use the Self-Assessment contents in your
presentations and materials for internal use and customers
without asking us - we are here to help.**

Trademarks

Many of the designations used by manufacturers and sellers to
distinguish their products are claimed as trademarks. Where those
designations appear in this book, and the publisher was aware of a
trademark claim, the designations appear as requested by the owner
of the trademark. All other product names and services identified
throughout this book are used in editorial fashion only and for the
benefit of such companies with no intention of infringement of the
trademark. No such use, or the use of any trade name, is intended to
convey endorsement or other affiliation with this book.

Table of Contents

About The Art of Service

The Art of Service, Business Process Architects since 2000, is dedicated to helping stakeholders achieve excellence.

Defining, designing, creating, and implementing a process to solve a stakeholders challenge or meet an objective is the most valuable role… In EVERY group, company, organization and department.

Unless you're talking a one-time, single-use project, there should be a process. Whether that process is managed and implemented by humans, AI, or a combination of the two, it needs to be designed by someone with a complex enough perspective to ask the right questions.

Someone capable of asking the right questions and step back and say, 'What are we really trying to accomplish here? And is there a different way to look at it?'

With The Art of Service's Standard Requirements Self-Assessments, we empower people who can do just that — whether their title is marketer, entrepreneur, manager, salesperson, consultant, Business Process Manager, executive assistant, IT Manager, CIO etc... —they are the people who rule the future. They are people who watch the process as it happens, and ask the right questions to make the process work better.

Contact us when you need any support with this Self-Assessment and any help with templates, blue-prints and examples of standard documents you might need:

http://theartofservice.com
service@theartofservice.com

Acknowledgments

This checklist was developed under the auspices of The Art of Service, chaired by Gerardus Blokdyk.

Representatives from several client companies participated in the preparation of this Self-Assessment.

In addition, we are thankful for the design and printing services provided.

Included Resources - how to access

Included with your purchase of the book is the Transforming Technology Self-Assessment Spreadsheet Dashboard which contains all questions and Self-Assessment areas and auto-generates insights, graphs, and project RACI planning - all with examples to get you started right away.

How? Simply send an email to
access@theartofservice.com
with this books' title in the subject to get the Transforming Technology Self Assessment Tool right away.

You will receive the following contents with New and Updated specific criteria:

- The latest quick edition of the book in PDF

- The latest complete edition of the book in PDF, which criteria correspond to the criteria in...

- The Self-Assessment Excel Dashboard, and...

- Example pre-filled Self-Assessment Excel Dashboard to get familiar with results generation

- In-depth specific Checklists covering the topic

- Project management checklists and templates to assist with implementation

INCLUDES LIFETIME SELF ASSESSMENT UPDATES

Every self assessment comes with Lifetime Updates and Lifetime Free Updated Books. Lifetime Updates is an industry-first feature which allows you to receive verified self assessment updates, ensuring you always have the most accurate information at your fingertips.

Get it now- you will be glad you did - do it now, before you forget.

Send an email to **access@theartofservice.com** with this books' title in the subject to get the Transforming Technology Self Assessment Tool right away.

Your feedback is invaluable to us

If you recently bought this book, we would love to hear from you! You can do this by writing a review on amazon (or the online store where you purchased this book) about your last purchase! As part of our continual service improvement process, we love to hear real client experiences and feedback.

How does it work?
To post a review on Amazon, just log in to your account and click on the Create Your Own Review button (under Customer Reviews) of the relevant product page. You can find examples of product reviews in Amazon. If you purchased from another online store, simply follow their procedures.

What happens when I submit my review?
Once you have submitted your review, send us an email at review@theartofservice.com with the link to your review so we can properly thank you for your feedback.

Purpose of this Self-Assessment

This Self-Assessment has been developed to improve understanding of the requirements and elements of Transforming Technology, based on best practices and standards in business process architecture, design and quality management.

It is designed to allow for a rapid Self-Assessment to determine how closely existing management practices and procedures correspond to the elements of the Self-Assessment.

The criteria of requirements and elements of Transforming Technology have been rephrased in the format of a Self-Assessment questionnaire, with a seven-criterion scoring system, as explained in this document.

In this format, even with limited background knowledge of

Transforming Technology, a manager can quickly review existing operations to determine how they measure up to the standards. This in turn can serve as the starting point of a 'gap analysis' to identify management tools or system elements that might usefully be implemented in the organization to help improve overall performance.

How to use the Self-Assessment

On the following pages are a series of questions to identify to what extent your Transforming Technology initiative is complete in comparison to the requirements set in standards.

To facilitate answering the questions, there is a space in front of each question to enter a score on a scale of '1' to '5'.

1 Strongly Disagree

2 Disagree

3 Neutral

4 Agree

5 Strongly Agree

Read the question and rate it with the following in front of mind:

'In my belief,
the answer to this question is clearly defined'.

There are two ways in which you can choose to interpret this statement;
1. how aware are you that the answer to the question is clearly defined
2. for more in-depth analysis you can choose to gather

evidence and confirm the answer to the question. This obviously will take more time, most Self-Assessment users opt for the first way to interpret the question and dig deeper later on based on the outcome of the overall Self-Assessment.

A score of '1' would mean that the answer is not clear at all, where a '5' would mean the answer is crystal clear and defined. Leave emtpy when the question is not applicable or you don't want to answer it, you can skip it without affecting your score. Write your score in the space provided.

After you have responded to all the appropriate statements in each section, compute your average score for that section, using the formula provided, and round to the nearest tenth. Then transfer to the corresponding spoke in the Transforming Technology Scorecard on the second next page of the Self-Assessment.

Your completed Transforming Technology Scorecard will give you a clear presentation of which Transforming Technology areas need attention.

Transforming Technology Scorecard Example

Example of how the finalized Scorecard can look like:

Transforming Technology Scorecard

Your Scores:

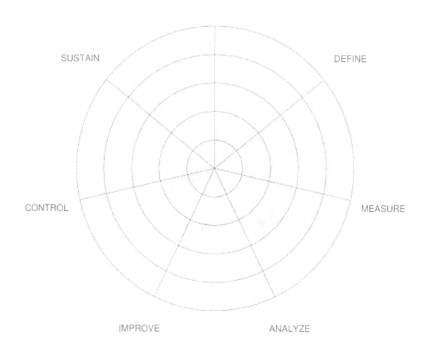

BEGINNING OF THE SELF-ASSESSMENT:

CRITERION #1: RECOGNIZE

INTENT: Be aware of the need for change. Recognize that there is an unfavorable variation, problem or symptom.

In my belief, the answer to this question is clearly defined:

5 Strongly Agree

4 Agree

3 Neutral

2 Disagree

1 Strongly Disagree

1. Are there regulatory / compliance issues?
<--- Score

2. Do you need to avoid or amend any transforming technology activities?
<--- Score

3. What activities does the governance board need to consider?

<--- Score

4. Are there any specific expectations or concerns about the transforming technology team, transforming technology itself?
<--- Score

5. For your transforming technology project, identify and describe the business environment, is there more than one layer to the business environment?
<--- Score

6. Would you recognize a threat from the inside?
<--- Score

7. How much are sponsors, customers, partners, stakeholders involved in transforming technology? In other words, what are the risks, if transforming technology does not deliver successfully?
<--- Score

8. What would happen if transforming technology weren't done?
<--- Score

9. Will new equipment/products be required to facilitate transforming technology delivery, for example is new software needed?
<--- Score

10. What are the expected benefits of transforming technology to the stakeholder?
<--- Score

11. How are the transforming technology's objectives aligned to the group's overall stakeholder strategy?

<--- Score

12. Who needs what information?
<--- Score

13. What are the timeframes required to resolve each of the issues/problems?
<--- Score

14. What are the transforming technology resources needed?
<--- Score

15. What are the minority interests and what amount of minority interests can be recognized?
<--- Score

16. What needs to be done?
<--- Score

17. Is it clear when you think of the day ahead of you what activities and tasks you need to complete?
<--- Score

18. What information do users need?
<--- Score

19. What else needs to be measured?
<--- Score

20. What situation(s) led to this transforming technology Self Assessment?
<--- Score

21. How does it fit into your organizational needs and

tasks?
<--- Score

22. Which information does the transforming technology business case need to include?
<--- Score

23. How do you assess your transforming technology workforce capability and capacity needs, including skills, competencies, and staffing levels?
<--- Score

24. Will transforming technology deliverables need to be tested and, if so, by whom?
<--- Score

25. How do you identify subcontractor relationships?
<--- Score

26. What does transforming technology success mean to the stakeholders?
<--- Score

27. Are there any revenue recognition issues?
<--- Score

28. What needs to stay?
<--- Score

29. When a transforming technology manager recognizes a problem, what options are available?
<--- Score

30. What are your needs in relation to transforming technology skills, labor, equipment, and markets?
<--- Score

31. How many trainings, in total, are needed?
<--- Score

32. Are your goals realistic? Do you need to redefine your problem? Perhaps the problem has changed or maybe you have reached your goal and need to set a new one?
<--- Score

33. Who else hopes to benefit from it?
<--- Score

34. Are you dealing with any of the same issues today as yesterday? What can you do about this?
<--- Score

35. How do you recognize an transforming technology objection?
<--- Score

36. What are the clients issues and concerns?
<--- Score

37. Does the problem have ethical dimensions?
<--- Score

38. Who needs to know about transforming technology?
<--- Score

39. Where do you need to exercise leadership?
<--- Score

40. What problems are you facing and how do you consider transforming technology will circumvent

those obstacles?
<--- Score

41. Will it solve real problems?
<--- Score

42. Which issues are too important to ignore?
<--- Score

43. As a sponsor, customer or management, how important is it to meet goals, objectives?
<--- Score

44. What tools and technologies are needed for a custom transforming technology project?
<--- Score

45. What prevents you from making the changes you know will make you a more effective transforming technology leader?
<--- Score

46. How are you going to measure success?
<--- Score

47. How are training requirements identified?
<--- Score

48. Whom do you really need or want to serve?
<--- Score

49. Are employees recognized for desired behaviors?
<--- Score

50. What transforming technology events should you

attend?
<--- Score

51. What transforming technology problem should be solved?
<--- Score

52. How do you take a forward-looking perspective in identifying transforming technology research related to market response and models?
<--- Score

53. How do you identify the kinds of information that you will need?
<--- Score

54. How can auditing be a preventative security measure?
<--- Score

55. What resources or support might you need?
<--- Score

56. What should be considered when identifying available resources, constraints, and deadlines?
<--- Score

57. What do employees need in the short term?
<--- Score

58. How do you recognize an objection?
<--- Score

59. Can management personnel recognize the monetary benefit of transforming technology?
<--- Score

60. Does transforming technology create potential expectations in other areas that need to be recognized and considered?
<--- Score

61. Think about the people you identified for your transforming technology project and the project responsibilities you would assign to them, what kind of training do you think they would need to perform these responsibilities effectively?
<--- Score

62. Who needs to know?
<--- Score

63. What do you need to start doing?
<--- Score

64. What is the extent or complexity of the transforming technology problem?
<--- Score

65. What vendors make products that address the transforming technology needs?
<--- Score

66. Are there recognized transforming technology problems?
<--- Score

67. Who defines the rules in relation to any given issue?
<--- Score

68. Are there transforming technology problems

defined?

<--- Score

69. Why is this needed?

<--- Score

70. Who needs budgets?

<--- Score

71. Looking at each person individually – does every one have the qualities which are needed to work in this group?

<--- Score

72. Are losses recognized in a timely manner?

<--- Score

73. Why the need?

<--- Score

74. What is the smallest subset of the problem you can usefully solve?

<--- Score

75. What creative shifts do you need to take?

<--- Score

76. Do you have/need 24-hour access to key personnel?

<--- Score

77. Do you need different information or graphics?

<--- Score

78. What is the transforming technology problem definition? What do you need to resolve?

<--- Score

79. Who should resolve the transforming technology issues?

<--- Score

80. Who are your key stakeholders who need to sign off?

<--- Score

81. Are controls defined to recognize and contain problems?

<--- Score

82. What transforming technology coordination do you need?

<--- Score

83. Do you recognize transforming technology achievements?

<--- Score

84. To what extent does each concerned units management team recognize transforming technology as an effective investment?

<--- Score

85. Does your organization need more transforming technology education?

<--- Score

86. Have you identified your transforming technology key performance indicators?

<--- Score

87. Did you miss any major transforming

technology issues?
<--- Score

88. What is the problem or issue?
<--- Score

89. Do you know what you need to know about transforming technology?
<--- Score

90. Will a response program recognize when a crisis occurs and provide some level of response?
<--- Score

91. What extra resources will you need?
<--- Score

92. Consider your own transforming technology project, what types of organizational problems do you think might be causing or affecting your problem, based on the work done so far?
<--- Score

93. What are the stakeholder objectives to be achieved with transforming technology?
<--- Score

94. Are employees recognized or rewarded for performance that demonstrates the highest levels of integrity?
<--- Score

95. What transforming technology capabilities do you need?
<--- Score

96. What is the problem and/or vulnerability?
<--- Score

97. Is it needed?
<--- Score

98. What is the recognized need?
<--- Score

99. Is the need for organizational change recognized?
<--- Score

Add up total points for this section:
_____ = Total points for this section

Divided by: _____ (number of
statements answered) = _____
Average score for this section

Transfer your score to the transforming
technology Index at the beginning of
the Self-Assessment.

CRITERION #2: DEFINE:

INTENT: Formulate the stakeholder problem. Define the problem, needs and objectives.

In my belief, the answer to this question is clearly defined:

5 Strongly Agree

4 Agree

3 Neutral

2 Disagree

1 Strongly Disagree

1. Has a project plan, Gantt chart, or similar been developed/completed?
<--- Score

2. What sources do you use to gather information for a transforming technology study?
<--- Score

3. What is the worst case scenario?

<--- Score

4. What critical content must be communicated –
who, what, when, where, and how?
<--- Score

5. Has a high-level 'as is' process map been completed,
verified and validated?
<--- Score

6. How do you gather transforming technology
requirements?
<--- Score

7. Is the team equipped with available and reliable
resources?
<--- Score

8. Who approved the transforming technology scope?
<--- Score

9. Are team charters developed?
<--- Score

10. Where can you gather more information?
<--- Score

11. Is there any additional transforming technology
definition of success?
<--- Score

12. Are stakeholder processes mapped?
<--- Score

**13. Are the transforming technology requirements
testable?**

<--- Score

14. Is scope creep really all bad news?
<--- Score

15. What transforming technology requirements should be gathered?
<--- Score

16. Who defines (or who defined) the rules and roles?
<--- Score

17. Is there regularly 100% attendance at the team meetings? If not, have appointed substitutes attended to preserve cross-functionality and full representation?
<--- Score

18. Do you have a transforming technology success story or case study ready to tell and share?
<--- Score

19. Is the team adequately staffed with the desired cross-functionality? If not, what additional resources are available to the team?
<--- Score

20. What is the context?
<--- Score

21. Who are the transforming technology improvement team members, including Management Leads and Coaches?
<--- Score

22. Is there a clear transforming technology case definition?
<--- Score

23. Has your scope been defined?
<--- Score

24. What intelligence can you gather?
<--- Score

25. How would you define the culture at your organization, how susceptible is it to transforming technology changes?
<--- Score

26. What is in the scope and what is not in scope?
<--- Score

27. Are audit criteria, scope, frequency and methods defined?
<--- Score

28. Has/have the customer(s) been identified?
<--- Score

29. Are customers identified and high impact areas defined?
<--- Score

30. What are the core elements of the transforming technology business case?
<--- Score

31. Has anyone else (internal or external to the group) attempted to solve this problem or a similar one before? If so, what knowledge can be leveraged from

these previous efforts?
<--- Score

32. Is there a critical path to deliver transforming technology results?
<--- Score

33. How do you manage scope?
<--- Score

34. What is the definition of success?
<--- Score

35. Do you have organizational privacy requirements?
<--- Score

36. Do the problem and goal statements meet the SMART criteria (specific, measurable, attainable, relevant, and time-bound)?
<--- Score

37. Does the team have regular meetings?
<--- Score

38. Are roles and responsibilities formally defined?
<--- Score

39. What are the transforming technology tasks and definitions?
<--- Score

40. Have specific policy objectives been defined?
<--- Score

41. How will variation in the actual durations of each activity be dealt with to ensure that the expected

transforming technology results are met?
<--- Score

42. Are accountability and ownership for transforming technology clearly defined?
<--- Score

43. What sort of initial information to gather?
<--- Score

44. What are the requirements for audit information?
<--- Score

45. How was the 'as is' process map developed, reviewed, verified and validated?
<--- Score

46. What is a worst-case scenario for losses?
<--- Score

47. What system do you use for gathering transforming technology information?
<--- Score

48. Scope of sensitive information?
<--- Score

49. Has a team charter been developed and communicated?
<--- Score

50. Are all requirements met?
<--- Score

51. What customer feedback methods were used to solicit their input?

<--- Score

52. What are the dynamics of the communication plan?
<--- Score

53. Are different versions of process maps needed to account for the different types of inputs?
<--- Score

54. How often are the team meetings?
<--- Score

55. In what way can you redefine the criteria of choice clients have in your category in your favor?
<--- Score

56. How do you gather the stories?
<--- Score

57. What is out of scope?
<--- Score

58. Is full participation by members in regularly held team meetings guaranteed?
<--- Score

59. What defines best in class?
<--- Score

60. What are the compelling stakeholder reasons for embarking on transforming technology?
<--- Score

61. If substitutes have been appointed, have they been briefed on the transforming technology goals

and received regular communications as to the progress to date?
<--- Score

62. Who is gathering information?
<--- Score

63. Is the transforming technology scope complete and appropriately sized?
<--- Score

64. Is the improvement team aware of the different versions of a process: what they think it is vs. what it actually is vs. what it should be vs. what it could be?
<--- Score

65. How do you catch transforming technology definition inconsistencies?
<--- Score

66. Is data collected and displayed to better understand customer(s) critical needs and requirements.
<--- Score

67. How do you manage changes in transforming technology requirements?
<--- Score

68. What is the scope?
<--- Score

69. What are (control) requirements for transforming technology Information?
<--- Score

70. How do you build the right business case?
<--- Score

71. What information do you gather?
<--- Score

72. Is the scope of transforming technology defined?
<--- Score

73. What scope do you want your strategy to cover?
<--- Score

74. The political context: who holds power?
<--- Score

75. Has the direction changed at all during the course of transforming technology? If so, when did it change and why?
<--- Score

76. What would be the goal or target for a transforming technology's improvement team?
<--- Score

77. Does the scope remain the same?
<--- Score

78. What happens if transforming technology's scope changes?
<--- Score

79. Are task requirements clearly defined?
<--- Score

80. What are the rough order estimates on cost savings/opportunities that transforming technology

brings?

<--- Score

81. When is/was the transforming technology start date?

<--- Score

82. Is there a completed, verified, and validated high-level 'as is' (not 'should be' or 'could be') stakeholder process map?

<--- Score

83. When is the estimated completion date?

<--- Score

84. Is the team sponsored by a champion or stakeholder leader?

<--- Score

85. What is the definition of transforming technology excellence?

<--- Score

86. Is the team formed and are team leaders (Coaches and Management Leads) assigned?

<--- Score

87. Are improvement team members fully trained on transforming technology?

<--- Score

88. What key stakeholder process output measure(s) does transforming technology leverage and how?

<--- Score

89. Will team members regularly document their

transforming technology work?
<--- Score

90. Are customer(s) identified and segmented according to their different needs and requirements?
<--- Score

91. What is the scope of the transforming technology work?
<--- Score

92. What is the scope of the transforming technology effort?
<--- Score

93. Will team members perform transforming technology work when assigned and in a timely fashion?
<--- Score

94. What are the Roles and Responsibilities for each team member and its leadership? Where is this documented?
<--- Score

95. Are approval levels defined for contracts and supplements to contracts?
<--- Score

96. What specifically is the problem? Where does it occur? When does it occur? What is its extent?
<--- Score

97. What are the record-keeping requirements of transforming technology activities?
<--- Score

98. What is out-of-scope initially?
<--- Score

99. When are meeting minutes sent out? Who is on the distribution list?
<--- Score

100. How do you manage unclear transforming technology requirements?
<--- Score

101. How are consistent transforming technology definitions important?
<--- Score

102. What baselines are required to be defined and managed?
<--- Score

103. Is a fully trained team formed, supported, and committed to work on the transforming technology improvements?
<--- Score

104. Is there a transforming technology management charter, including stakeholder case, problem and goal statements, scope, milestones, roles and responsibilities, communication plan?
<--- Score

105. How and when will the baselines be defined?
<--- Score

106. How do you keep key subject matter experts in the loop?

<--- Score

107. How does the transforming technology manager ensure against scope creep?
<--- Score

108. What information should you gather?
<--- Score

109. How did the transforming technology manager receive input to the development of a transforming technology improvement plan and the estimated completion dates/times of each activity?
<--- Score

110. Is transforming technology currently on schedule according to the plan?
<--- Score

111. How do you think the partners involved in transforming technology would have defined success?
<--- Score

112. Is there a completed SIPOC representation, describing the Suppliers, Inputs, Process, Outputs, and Customers?
<--- Score

113. Is the transforming technology scope manageable?
<--- Score

114. Has the transforming technology work been fairly and/or equitably divided and delegated among team members who are qualified and capable to

perform the work? Has everyone contributed?
<--- Score

115. Is transforming technology linked to key stakeholder goals and objectives?
<--- Score

116. What was the context?
<--- Score

117. Have all of the relationships been defined properly?
<--- Score

118. How can the value of transforming technology be defined?
<--- Score

119. What gets examined?
<--- Score

120. How would you define transforming technology leadership?
<--- Score

121. Have the customer needs been translated into specific, measurable requirements? How?
<--- Score

122. What constraints exist that might impact the team?
<--- Score

123. Who is gathering transforming technology information?
<--- Score

124. What is in scope?
<--- Score

125. Are there different segments of customers?
<--- Score

126. What are the transforming technology use cases?
<--- Score

127. Do you all define transforming technology in the same way?
<--- Score

128. Are the transforming technology requirements complete?
<--- Score

129. Has everyone on the team, including the team leaders, been properly trained?
<--- Score

130. How do you hand over transforming technology context?
<--- Score

131. What are the tasks and definitions?
<--- Score

132. Will a transforming technology production readiness review be required?
<--- Score

133. Why are you doing transforming technology and what is the scope?
<--- Score

134. How will the transforming technology team and the group measure complete success of transforming technology?
<--- Score

135. Is transforming technology required?
<--- Score

136. Has the improvement team collected the 'voice of the customer' (obtained feedback – qualitative and quantitative)?
<--- Score

137. How have you defined all transforming technology requirements first?
<--- Score

138. Is the current 'as is' process being followed? If not, what are the discrepancies?
<--- Score

139. How is the team tracking and documenting its work?
<--- Score

140. Are there any constraints known that bear on the ability to perform transforming technology work? How is the team addressing them?
<--- Score

141. Is it clearly defined in and to your organization what you do?
<--- Score

142. What are the boundaries of the scope? What is in

bounds and what is not? What is the start point? What is the stop point?

<--- Score

Add up total points for this section:
_____ = Total points for this section

Divided by: _____ (number of statements answered) = _____
Average score for this section

Transfer your score to the transforming technology Index at the beginning of the Self-Assessment.

CRITERION #3: MEASURE:

INTENT: Gather the correct data.
Measure the current performance and
evolution of the situation.

In my belief, the answer to this
question is clearly defined:

5 Strongly Agree

4 Agree

3 Neutral

2 Disagree

1 Strongly Disagree

1. Where is the cost?
<--- Score

2. What are your primary costs, revenues, assets?
<--- Score

3. What would it cost to replace your technology?
<--- Score

4. Is data collected on key measures that were identified?
<--- Score

5. What is measured? Why?
<--- Score

6. Are supply costs steady or fluctuating?
<--- Score

7. What can be used to verify compliance?
<--- Score

8. How will costs be allocated?
<--- Score

9. Do the benefits outweigh the costs?
<--- Score

10. Is a follow-up focused external transforming technology review required?
<--- Score

11. How sensitive must the transforming technology strategy be to cost?
<--- Score

12. How do you identify and analyze stakeholders and their interests?
<--- Score

13. How will success or failure be measured?
<--- Score

14. Is the cost worth the transforming technology effort ?

<--- Score

15. Are there measurements based on task performance?
<--- Score

16. What are the costs of delaying transforming technology action?
<--- Score

17. How can you measure transforming technology in a systematic way?
<--- Score

18. What does losing customers cost your organization?
<--- Score

19. Who participated in the data collection for measurements?
<--- Score

20. What are the agreed upon definitions of the high impact areas, defect(s), unit(s), and opportunities that will figure into the process capability metrics?
<--- Score

21. What are predictive transforming technology analytics?
<--- Score

22. How is the value delivered by transforming technology being measured?
<--- Score

23. What is the right balance of time and resources

between investigation, analysis, and discussion and dissemination?
<--- Score

24. What are the strategic priorities for this year?
<--- Score

25. Which measures and indicators matter?
<--- Score

26. How can a transforming technology test verify your ideas or assumptions?
<--- Score

27. Who should receive measurement reports?
<--- Score

28. What are hidden transforming technology quality costs?
<--- Score

29. How are costs allocated?
<--- Score

30. Do you have any cost transforming technology limitation requirements?
<--- Score

31. Are you taking your company in the direction of better and revenue or cheaper and cost?
<--- Score

32. What are your customers expectations and measures?
<--- Score

33. What are the key input variables? What are the key process variables? What are the key output variables?
<--- Score

34. What drives O&M cost?
<--- Score

35. What are the transforming technology investment costs?
<--- Score

36. Is long term and short term variability accounted for?
<--- Score

37. How do you aggregate measures across priorities?
<--- Score

38. What are the current costs of the transforming technology process?
<--- Score

39. How will measures be used to manage and adapt?
<--- Score

40. How do you verify your resources?
<--- Score

41. When should you bother with diagrams?
<--- Score

42. What charts has the team used to display the components of variation in the process?
<--- Score

43. How will the transforming technology data be analyzed?
<--- Score

44. How do you verify and validate the transforming technology data?
<--- Score

45. How do your measurements capture actionable transforming technology information for use in exceeding your customers expectations and securing your customers engagement?
<--- Score

46. How can you reduce costs?
<--- Score

47. What evidence is there and what is measured?
<--- Score

48. How do you verify performance?
<--- Score

49. What are the estimated costs of proposed changes?
<--- Score

50. What does your operating model cost?
<--- Score

51. Is there an opportunity to verify requirements?
<--- Score

52. What is the root cause(s) of the problem?
<--- Score

53. Does transforming technology analysis isolate the fundamental causes of problems?

<--- Score

54. What is your transforming technology quality cost segregation study?

<--- Score

55. What methods are feasible and acceptable to estimate the impact of reforms?

<--- Score

56. Was a data collection plan established?

<--- Score

57. Are transforming technology vulnerabilities categorized and prioritized?

<--- Score

58. What kind of analytics data will be gathered?

<--- Score

59. What disadvantage does this cause for the user?

<--- Score

60. Why do you expend time and effort to implement measurement, for whom?

<--- Score

61. How will you measure your transforming technology effectiveness?

<--- Score

62. Did you tackle the cause or the symptom?

<--- Score

63. What are you verifying?
<--- Score

64. What could cause delays in the schedule?
<--- Score

65. How do you prevent mis-estimating cost?
<--- Score

66. How can you measure the performance?
<--- Score

67. What relevant entities could be measured?
<--- Score

68. Will transforming technology have an impact on current business continuity, disaster recovery processes and/or infrastructure?
<--- Score

69. What is an unallowable cost?
<--- Score

70. What could cause you to change course?
<--- Score

71. What is your cost benefit analysis?
<--- Score

72. What particular quality tools did the team find helpful in establishing measurements?
<--- Score

73. Does a transforming technology quantification method exist?
<--- Score

74. Are actual costs in line with budgeted costs?
<--- Score

75. What causes innovation to fail or succeed in your organization?
<--- Score

76. Was a business case (cost/benefit) developed?
<--- Score

77. How will your organization measure success?
<--- Score

78. What do people want to verify?
<--- Score

79. Do you effectively measure and reward individual and team performance?
<--- Score

80. How frequently do you track transforming technology measures?
<--- Score

81. What key measures identified indicate the performance of the stakeholder process?
<--- Score

82. What are your key transforming technology organizational performance measures, including key short and longer-term financial measures?
<--- Score

83. What data was collected (past, present, future/ongoing)?

<--- Score

84. What tests verify requirements?
<--- Score

85. At what cost?
<--- Score

86. Are indirect costs charged to the transforming technology program?
<--- Score

87. Does the transforming technology task fit the client's priorities?
<--- Score

88. Have you found any 'ground fruit' or 'low-hanging fruit' for immediate remedies to the gap in performance?
<--- Score

89. Has a cost center been established?
<--- Score

90. Are missed transforming technology opportunities costing your organization money?
<--- Score

91. Is the solution cost-effective?
<--- Score

92. Are the transforming technology benefits worth its costs?
<--- Score

93. Can you measure the return on analysis?

<--- Score

94. The approach of traditional transforming technology works for detail complexity but is focused on a systematic approach rather than an understanding of the nature of systems themselves, what approach will permit your organization to deal with the kind of unpredictable emergent behaviors that dynamic complexity can introduce?
<--- Score

95. Is Process Variation Displayed/Communicated?
<--- Score

96. Are losses documented, analyzed, and remedial processes developed to prevent future losses?
<--- Score

97. What are the operational costs after transforming technology deployment?
<--- Score

98. How do you measure variability?
<--- Score

99. Have all non-recommended alternatives been analyzed in sufficient detail?
<--- Score

100. How will effects be measured?
<--- Score

101. What measurements are possible, practicable and meaningful?
<--- Score

102. What are the costs of reform?
<--- Score

103. Have you made assumptions about the shape of the future, particularly its impact on your customers and competitors?
<--- Score

104. Among the transforming technology product and service cost to be estimated, which is considered hardest to estimate?
<--- Score

105. How do you stay flexible and focused to recognize larger transforming technology results?
<--- Score

106. What are allowable costs?
<--- Score

107. How do you measure lifecycle phases?
<--- Score

108. Have you included everything in your transforming technology cost models?
<--- Score

109. What do you measure and why?
<--- Score

110. Do you verify that corrective actions were taken?
<--- Score

111. When a disaster occurs, who gets priority?
<--- Score

112. Have the types of risks that may impact transforming technology been identified and analyzed?
<--- Score

113. When are costs are incurred?
<--- Score

114. Do you have a flow diagram of what happens?
<--- Score

115. Are key measures identified and agreed upon?
<--- Score

116. Was a life-cycle cost analysis performed?
<--- Score

117. What is the total cost related to deploying transforming technology, including any consulting or professional services?
<--- Score

118. What causes investor action?
<--- Score

119. How do you verify if transforming technology is built right?
<--- Score

120. What is the total fixed cost?
<--- Score

121. How do you do risk analysis of rare, cascading, catastrophic events?
<--- Score

122. How are you verifying it?
<--- Score

123. Where can you go to verify the info?
<--- Score

124. How do you know that any transforming
technology analysis is complete and comprehensive?
<--- Score

125. Is key measure data collection planned
and executed, process variation displayed and
communicated and performance baselined?
<--- Score

126. Do staff have the necessary skills to collect,
analyze, and report data?
<--- Score

127. How to cause the change?
<--- Score

128. How is progress measured?
<--- Score

129. Does transforming technology systematically
track and analyze outcomes for accountability and
quality improvement?
<--- Score

130. What causes extra work or rework?
<--- Score

131. Are the measurements objective?
<--- Score

132. How do you verify the authenticity of the data and information used?
<--- Score

133. How do you verify the transforming technology requirements quality?
<--- Score

134. Are high impact defects defined and identified in the stakeholder process?
<--- Score

135. How do you verify and develop ideas and innovations?
<--- Score

136. What has the team done to assure the stability and accuracy of the measurement process?
<--- Score

137. What is the cost of rework?
<--- Score

138. Does transforming technology analysis show the relationships among important transforming technology factors?
<--- Score

139. Which transforming technology impacts are significant?
<--- Score

140. What does verifying compliance entail?
<--- Score

141. Are you able to realize any cost savings?

<--- Score

142. How does cost-to-serve analysis help?
<--- Score

143. Who pays the cost?
<--- Score

144. Are process variation components displayed/
communicated using suitable charts, graphs, plots?
<--- Score

145. How do you quantify and qualify impacts?
<--- Score

146. How much does it cost?
<--- Score

147. What harm might be caused?
<--- Score

148. Is a solid data collection plan established that
includes measurement systems analysis?
<--- Score

**149. Which stakeholder characteristics are
analyzed?**
<--- Score

150. Have design-to-cost goals been established?
<--- Score

151. Can you do transforming technology without
complex (expensive) analysis?
<--- Score

152. How do you verify transforming technology completeness and accuracy?

<--- Score

153. What is the cause of any transforming technology gaps?

<--- Score

154. What are your operating costs?

<--- Score

155. Is it possible to estimate the impact of unanticipated complexity such as wrong or failed assumptions, feedback, etcetera on proposed reforms?

<--- Score

156. What causes mismanagement?

<--- Score

157. How do you measure success?

<--- Score

158. What are the costs?

<--- Score

159. Has a cost benefit analysis been performed?

<--- Score

160. What measurements are being captured?

<--- Score

161. Have changes been properly/adequately analyzed for effect?

<--- Score

162. Does your organization systematically track and analyze outcomes related for accountability and quality improvement?
<--- Score

163. Have the concerns of stakeholders to help identify and define potential barriers been obtained and analyzed?
<--- Score

164. Is data collection planned and executed?
<--- Score

165. What potential environmental factors impact the transforming technology effort?
<--- Score

166. Which costs should be taken into account?
<--- Score

167. What are the types and number of measures to use?
<--- Score

168. What happens if cost savings do not materialize?
<--- Score

169. What details are required of the transforming technology cost structure?
<--- Score

170. Who is involved in verifying compliance?
<--- Score

171. Are you aware of what could cause a problem?

<--- Score

172. Why a transforming technology focus?
<--- Score

173. What are the transforming technology key cost drivers?
<--- Score

174. What are your key transforming technology indicators that you will measure, analyze and track?
<--- Score

175. What is your decision requirements diagram?
<--- Score

176. Do you aggressively reward and promote the people who have the biggest impact on creating excellent transforming technology services/products?
<--- Score

177. How frequently do you verify your transforming technology strategy?
<--- Score

178. Are there competing transforming technology priorities?
<--- Score

179. How will you measure success?
<--- Score

180. How large is the gap between current performance and the customer-specified (goal) performance?
<--- Score

181. How do you control the overall costs of your work processes?
<--- Score

182. What are the costs and benefits?
<--- Score

183. Is there a Performance Baseline?
<--- Score

184. How are measurements made?
<--- Score

185. When is Root Cause Analysis Required?
<--- Score

186. How can you reduce the costs of obtaining inputs?
<--- Score

187. Why do the measurements/indicators matter?
<--- Score

188. What does a Test Case verify?
<--- Score

189. Where is it measured?
<--- Score

Add up total points for this section:

_ _ _ _ _ = Total points for this section

Divided by: _ _ _ _ _ _ (number of
statements answered) = _ _ _ _ _ _
Average score for this section

Transfer your score to the transforming
technology Index at the beginning of
the Self-Assessment.

CRITERION #4: ANALYZE:

INTENT: Analyze causes, assumptions and hypotheses.

In my belief, the answer to this question is clearly defined:

5 Strongly Agree

4 Agree

3 Neutral

2 Disagree

1 Strongly Disagree

1. Are all staff in core transforming technology subjects Highly Qualified?
<--- Score

2. What is the oversight process?
<--- Score

3. What is the transforming technology Driver?
<--- Score

4. What were the crucial 'moments of truth' on the process map?
<--- Score

5. What successful thing are you doing today that may be blinding you to new growth opportunities?
<--- Score

6. Are your outputs consistent?
<--- Score

7. Should you invest in industry-recognized qualifications?
<--- Score

8. Do you, as a leader, bounce back quickly from setbacks?
<--- Score

9. What is the Value Stream Mapping?
<--- Score

10. How is the data gathered?
<--- Score

11. Do your employees have the opportunity to do what they do best everyday?
<--- Score

12. Have the problem and goal statements been updated to reflect the additional knowledge gained from the analyze phase?
<--- Score

13. What training and qualifications will you need?
<--- Score

14. What tools were used to narrow the list of possible causes?
<--- Score

15. Were Pareto charts (or similar) used to portray the 'heavy hitters' (or key sources of variation)?
<--- Score

16. How is the transforming technology Value Stream Mapping managed?
<--- Score

17. Have you defined which data is gathered how?
<--- Score

18. Is the performance gap determined?
<--- Score

19. Is pre-qualification of suppliers carried out?
<--- Score

20. What quality tools were used to get through the analyze phase?
<--- Score

21. A compounding model resolution with available relevant data can often provide insight towards a solution methodology; which transforming technology models, tools and techniques are necessary?
<--- Score

22. Do you understand your management processes today?
<--- Score

23. Who is involved with workflow mapping?
<--- Score

24. Have any additional benefits been identified that will result from closing all or most of the gaps?
<--- Score

25. Is there an established change management process?
<--- Score

26. What other organizational variables, such as reward systems or communication systems, affect the performance of this transforming technology process?
<--- Score

27. How much data can be collected in the given timeframe?
<--- Score

28. What output to create?
<--- Score

29. What were the financial benefits resulting from any 'ground fruit or low-hanging fruit' (quick fixes)?
<--- Score

30. Do quality systems drive continuous improvement?
<--- Score

31. Was a cause-and-effect diagram used to explore the different types of causes (or sources of variation)?
<--- Score

32. What tools were used to generate the list of possible causes?
<--- Score

33. What are the disruptive transforming technology technologies that enable your organization to radically change your business processes?
<--- Score

34. What are your key performance measures or indicators and in-process measures for the control and improvement of your transforming technology processes?
<--- Score

35. What methods do you use to gather transforming technology data?
<--- Score

36. Is there a strict change management process?
<--- Score

37. What is the complexity of the output produced?
<--- Score

38. How can risk management be tied procedurally to process elements?
<--- Score

39. Think about the functions involved in your transforming technology project, what processes flow from these functions?
<--- Score

40. What are your best practices for minimizing transforming technology project risk, while demonstrating incremental value and quick wins throughout the transforming technology project lifecycle?
<--- Score

41. How does the organization define, manage, and improve its transforming technology processes?
<--- Score

42. How do you implement and manage your work processes to ensure that they meet design requirements?
<--- Score

43. Was a detailed process map created to amplify critical steps of the 'as is' stakeholder process?
<--- Score

44. What are the personnel training and qualifications required?
<--- Score

45. What are the transforming technology business drivers?
<--- Score

46. What data is gathered?
<--- Score

47. Record-keeping requirements flow from the records needed as inputs, outputs, controls and for transformation of a transforming technology process, are the records needed as inputs to the transforming technology process available?

<--- Score

48. How do your work systems and key work processes relate to and capitalize on your core competencies?
<--- Score

49. Who will gather what data?
<--- Score

50. Who gets your output?
<--- Score

51. What resources go in to get the desired output?
<--- Score

52. What are your transforming technology processes?
<--- Score

53. What qualifies as competition?
<--- Score

54. What is your organizations process which leads to recognition of value generation?
<--- Score

55. Who is involved in the management review process?
<--- Score

56. What process improvements will be needed?
<--- Score

57. What is the output?
<--- Score

58. Are gaps between current performance and the goal performance identified?
<--- Score

59. How do mission and objectives affect the transforming technology processes of your organization?
<--- Score

60. Are transforming technology changes recognized early enough to be approved through the regular process?
<--- Score

61. Is data and process analysis, root cause analysis and quantifying the gap/opportunity in place?
<--- Score

62. How do you use transforming technology data and information to support organizational decision making and innovation?
<--- Score

63. What transforming technology data should be collected?
<--- Score

64. What, related to, transforming technology processes does your organization outsource?
<--- Score

65. What process should you select for improvement?
<--- Score

66. What do you need to qualify?

<--- Score

67. What will drive transforming technology change?
<--- Score

68. How is transforming technology data gathered?
<--- Score

69. What qualifications do transforming technology leaders need?
<--- Score

70. How will the transforming technology data be captured?
<--- Score

71. How difficult is it to qualify what transforming technology ROI is?
<--- Score

72. What information qualified as important?
<--- Score

73. What are the revised rough estimates of the financial savings/opportunity for transforming technology improvements?
<--- Score

74. How do you ensure that the transforming technology opportunity is realistic?
<--- Score

75. What qualifications are needed?
<--- Score

76. Which transforming technology data should be retained?

<--- Score

77. What conclusions were drawn from the team's data collection and analysis? How did the team reach these conclusions?

<--- Score

78. Do you have the authority to produce the output?

<--- Score

79. What qualifications and skills do you need?

<--- Score

80. Is the required transforming technology data gathered?

<--- Score

81. Is the suppliers process defined and controlled?

<--- Score

82. Has an output goal been set?

<--- Score

83. What types of data do your transforming technology indicators require?

<--- Score

84. What data do you need to collect?

<--- Score

85. What is the cost of poor quality as supported by the team's analysis?

<--- Score

86. Is the transforming technology process severely broken such that a re-design is necessary?
<--- Score

87. What does the data say about the performance of the stakeholder process?
<--- Score

88. How do you promote understanding that opportunity for improvement is not criticism of the status quo, or the people who created the status quo?
<--- Score

89. Are you missing transforming technology opportunities?
<--- Score

90. Is the gap/opportunity displayed and communicated in financial terms?
<--- Score

91. Is the final output clearly identified?
<--- Score

92. What are your current levels and trends in key measures or indicators of transforming technology product and process performance that are important to and directly serve your customers? How do these results compare with the performance of your competitors and other organizations with similar offerings?
<--- Score

93. An organizationally feasible system request is one that considers the mission, goals and objectives of the

organization, key questions are: is the transforming technology solution request practical and will it solve a problem or take advantage of an opportunity to achieve company goals?

<--- Score

94. Has data output been validated?

<--- Score

95. What is your organizations system for selecting qualified vendors?

<--- Score

96. Are all team members qualified for all tasks?

<--- Score

97. Identify an operational issue in your organization, for example, could a particular task be done more quickly or more efficiently by transforming technology?

<--- Score

98. What did the team gain from developing a sub-process map?

<--- Score

99. Think about some of the processes you undertake within your organization, which do you own?

<--- Score

100. How are outputs preserved and protected?

<--- Score

101. Did any additional data need to be collected?

<--- Score

102. How do you measure the operational performance of your key work systems and processes, including productivity, cycle time, and other appropriate measures of process effectiveness, efficiency, and innovation?
<--- Score

103. Do staff qualifications match your project?
<--- Score

104. Did any value-added analysis or 'lean thinking' take place to identify some of the gaps shown on the 'as is' process map?
<--- Score

105. What other jobs or tasks affect the performance of the steps in the transforming technology process?
<--- Score

106. How is the way you as the leader think and process information affecting your organizational culture?
<--- Score

107. What are your current levels and trends in key transforming technology measures or indicators of product and process performance that are important to and directly serve your customers?
<--- Score

108. What kind of crime could a potential new hire have committed that would not only not disqualify him/her from being hired by your organization, but would actually indicate that he/she might be a particularly good fit?
<--- Score

109. What transforming technology metrics are outputs of the process?
<--- Score

110. What transforming technology data do you gather or use now?
<--- Score

111. How was the detailed process map generated, verified, and validated?
<--- Score

112. Who qualifies to gain access to data?
<--- Score

113. Were any designed experiments used to generate additional insight into the data analysis?
<--- Score

114. How do you identify specific transforming technology investment opportunities and emerging trends?
<--- Score

115. What are evaluation criteria for the output?
<--- Score

116. How will the change process be managed?
<--- Score

117. Were there any improvement opportunities identified from the process analysis?
<--- Score

118. Can you add value to the current transforming

technology decision-making process (largely qualitative) by incorporating uncertainty modeling (more quantitative)?
<--- Score

119. What internal processes need improvement?
<--- Score

120. What are the necessary qualifications?
<--- Score

121. What are your outputs?
<--- Score

122. What are the best opportunities for value improvement?
<--- Score

123. Where can you get qualified talent today?
<--- Score

124. How often will data be collected for measures?
<--- Score

125. Who owns what data?
<--- Score

Add up total points for this section:
_ _ _ _ _ = Total points for this section

Divided by: _ _ _ _ _ _ (number of statements answered) = _ _ _ _ _ _
Average score for this section

Transfer your score to the transforming

technology Index at the beginning of
the Self-Assessment.

CRITERION #5: IMPROVE:

INTENT: Develop a practical solution.
Innovate, establish and test the
solution and to measure the results.

In my belief, the answer to this
question is clearly defined:

5 Strongly Agree

4 Agree

3 Neutral

2 Disagree

1 Strongly Disagree

1. How risky is your organization?
<--- Score

**2. Is there a high likelihood that any
recommendations will achieve their intended
results?**
<--- Score

3. How do you improve your likelihood of success ?

<--- Score

4. Which transforming technology solution is appropriate?
<--- Score

5. Where do the transforming technology decisions reside?
<--- Score

6. How scalable is your transforming technology solution?
<--- Score

7. When you map the key players in your own work and the types/domains of relationships with them, which relationships do you find easy and which challenging, and why?
<--- Score

8. How does the solution remove the key sources of issues discovered in the analyze phase?
<--- Score

9. Who will be responsible for making the decisions to include or exclude requested changes once transforming technology is underway?
<--- Score

10. How does your organization evaluate strategic transforming technology success?
<--- Score

11. How do you keep improving transforming technology?
<--- Score

12. What went well, what should change, what can improve?
<--- Score

13. Is there a cost/benefit analysis of optimal solution(s)?
<--- Score

14. What is the transforming technology's sustainability risk?
<--- Score

15. For decision problems, how do you develop a decision statement?
<--- Score

16. At what point will vulnerability assessments be performed once transforming technology is put into production (e.g., ongoing Risk Management after implementation)?
<--- Score

17. What is the team's contingency plan for potential problems occurring in implementation?
<--- Score

18. Does a good decision guarantee a good outcome?
<--- Score

19. How do you link measurement and risk?
<--- Score

20. How do you improve transforming technology service perception, and satisfaction?
<--- Score

21. Are events managed to resolution?
<--- Score

22. Is there a small-scale pilot for proposed improvement(s)? What conclusions were drawn from the outcomes of a pilot?
<--- Score

23. How are transforming technology risks managed?
<--- Score

24. How will you measure the results?
<--- Score

25. Is supporting transforming technology documentation required?
<--- Score

26. What were the criteria for evaluating a transforming technology pilot?
<--- Score

27. Is a solution implementation plan established, including schedule/work breakdown structure, resources, risk management plan, cost/budget, and control plan?
<--- Score

28. How significant is the improvement in the eyes of the end user?
<--- Score

29. Is the transforming technology risk managed?
<--- Score

30. In the past few months, what is the smallest change you have made that has had the biggest positive result? What was it about that small change that produced the large return?
<--- Score

31. Are risk triggers captured?
<--- Score

32. Do vendor agreements bring new compliance risk ?
<--- Score

33. What are your current levels and trends in key measures or indicators of workforce and leader development?
<--- Score

34. What criteria will you use to assess your transforming technology risks?
<--- Score

35. What do you want to improve?
<--- Score

36. How do you go about comparing transforming technology approaches/solutions?
<--- Score

37. What attendant changes will need to be made to ensure that the solution is successful?
<--- Score

38. Risk factors: what are the characteristics of transforming technology that make it risky?

<--- Score

39. Who should make the transforming technology decisions?
<--- Score

40. What needs improvement? Why?
<--- Score

41. Was a pilot designed for the proposed solution(s)?
<--- Score

42. What strategies for transforming technology improvement are successful?
<--- Score

43. Which of the recognised risks out of all risks can be most likely transferred?
<--- Score

44. How can you improve performance?
<--- Score

45. Who controls the risk?
<--- Score

46. What is transforming technology's impact on utilizing the best solution(s)?
<--- Score

47. Is the solution technically practical?
<--- Score

48. To what extent does management recognize transforming technology as a tool to increase the results?

<--- Score

49. Is the scope clearly documented?
<--- Score

50. Would you develop a transforming technology Communication Strategy?
<--- Score

51. Who makes the transforming technology decisions in your organization?
<--- Score

52. What tools were used to tap into the creativity and encourage 'outside the box' thinking?
<--- Score

53. Was a transforming technology charter developed?
<--- Score

54. What are the affordable transforming technology risks?
<--- Score

55. Do those selected for the transforming technology team have a good general understanding of what transforming technology is all about?
<--- Score

56. What is the risk?
<--- Score

57. How do you deal with transforming technology risk?
<--- Score

58. What is the implementation plan?
<--- Score

59. What can you do to improve?
<--- Score

60. How will the team or the process owner(s) monitor the implementation plan to see that it is working as intended?
<--- Score

61. What area needs the greatest improvement?
<--- Score

62. What are the concrete transforming technology results?
<--- Score

63. Can the solution be designed and implemented within an acceptable time period?
<--- Score

64. Are you assessing transforming technology and risk?
<--- Score

65. What is the magnitude of the improvements?
<--- Score

66. What tools were most useful during the improve phase?
<--- Score

67. What were the underlying assumptions on the cost-benefit analysis?

<--- Score

68. How will you know when its improved?
<--- Score

69. Who are the people involved in developing and implementing transforming technology?
<--- Score

70. What tools were used to evaluate the potential solutions?
<--- Score

71. transforming technology risk decisions: whose call Is It?
<--- Score

72. Are new and improved process ('should be') maps developed?
<--- Score

73. What resources are required for the improvement efforts?
<--- Score

74. How can you better manage risk?
<--- Score

75. How did the team generate the list of possible solutions?
<--- Score

76. Explorations of the frontiers of transforming technology will help you build influence, improve transforming technology, optimize decision making, and sustain change, what is your approach?

<--- Score

77. How do you manage transforming technology risk?
<--- Score

78. Is a contingency plan established?
<--- Score

79. Is the measure of success for transforming technology understandable to a variety of people?
<--- Score

80. What transforming technology improvements can be made?
<--- Score

81. How do you mitigate transforming technology risk?
<--- Score

82. Have you achieved transforming technology improvements?
<--- Score

83. Do you combine technical expertise with business knowledge and transforming technology Key topics include lifecycles, development approaches, requirements and how to make a business case?
<--- Score

84. Where do you need transforming technology improvement?
<--- Score

85. Have you identified breakpoints and/or risk

tolerances that will trigger broad consideration of a potential need for intervention or modification of strategy?

<--- Score

86. Who will be using the results of the measurement activities?

<--- Score

87. What practices helps your organization to develop its capacity to recognize patterns?

<--- Score

88. How can the phases of transforming technology development be identified?

<--- Score

89. Who are the key stakeholders for the transforming technology evaluation?

<--- Score

90. Is pilot data collected and analyzed?

<--- Score

91. How do the transforming technology results compare with the performance of your competitors and other organizations with similar offerings?

<--- Score

92. How will the group know that the solution worked?

<--- Score

93. Are decisions made in a timely manner?

<--- Score

94. If you could go back in time five years, what decision would you make differently? What is your best guess as to what decision you're making today you might regret five years from now?
<--- Score

95. What should a proof of concept or pilot accomplish?
<--- Score

96. How can you improve transforming technology?
<--- Score

97. How are policy decisions made and where?
<--- Score

98. What communications are necessary to support the implementation of the solution?
<--- Score

99. How will you recognize and celebrate results?
<--- Score

100. Is any transforming technology documentation required?
<--- Score

101. Does the goal represent a desired result that can be measured?
<--- Score

102. Is the transforming technology documentation thorough?
<--- Score

103. What actually has to improve and by how much?

<--- Score

104. Are improved process ('should be') maps modified based on pilot data and analysis?
<--- Score

105. Do you need to do a usability evaluation?
<--- Score

106. How do you measure risk?
<--- Score

107. Is the implementation plan designed?
<--- Score

108. Is risk periodically assessed?
<--- Score

109. Were any criteria developed to assist the team in testing and evaluating potential solutions?
<--- Score

110. Who manages transforming technology risk?
<--- Score

111. What does the 'should be' process map/design look like?
<--- Score

112. Is the optimal solution selected based on testing and analysis?
<--- Score

113. What tools do you use once you have decided on a transforming technology strategy and more importantly how do you choose?

<--- Score

114. Can you identify any significant risks or exposures to transforming technology third- parties (vendors, service providers, alliance partners etc) that concern you?
<--- Score

115. What error proofing will be done to address some of the discrepancies observed in the 'as is' process?
<--- Score

116. Why improve in the first place?
<--- Score

117. Risk events: what are the things that could go wrong?
<--- Score

118. How do you improve productivity?
<--- Score

119. Describe the design of the pilot and what tests were conducted, if any?
<--- Score

120. Are there any constraints (technical, political, cultural, or otherwise) that would inhibit certain solutions?
<--- Score

121. How does the team improve its work?
<--- Score

122. Who will be responsible for documenting the transforming technology requirements in detail?

<--- Score

123. How do you manage and improve your transforming technology work systems to deliver customer value and achieve organizational success and sustainability?
<--- Score

124. Risk Identification: What are the possible risk events your organization faces in relation to transforming technology?
<--- Score

125. Are the best solutions selected?
<--- Score

126. Who controls key decisions that will be made?
<--- Score

127. What are the implications of the one critical transforming technology decision 10 minutes, 10 months, and 10 years from now?
<--- Score

128. Do you cover the five essential competencies: Communication, Collaboration,Innovation, Adaptability, and Leadership that improve an organizations ability to leverage the new transforming technology in a volatile global economy?
<--- Score

129. What lessons, if any, from a pilot were incorporated into the design of the full-scale solution?
<--- Score

130. How will you know that you have improved?

<--- Score

131. For estimation problems, how do you develop an estimation statement?
<--- Score

132. What improvements have been achieved?
<--- Score

133. How do you define the solutions' scope?
<--- Score

134. What risks do you need to manage?
<--- Score

135. What are the expected transforming technology results?
<--- Score

136. What to do with the results or outcomes of measurements?
<--- Score

137. Who do you report transforming technology results to?
<--- Score

138. How can skill-level changes improve transforming technology?
<--- Score

139. How do you decide how much to remunerate an employee?
<--- Score

140. Will the controls trigger any other risks?

<--- Score

141. How do you measure progress and evaluate training effectiveness?
<--- Score

142. How will you know that a change is an improvement?
<--- Score

143. Are possible solutions generated and tested?
<--- Score

Add up total points for this section:
_ _ _ _ _ = Total points for this section

Divided by: _ _ _ _ _ _ (number of statements answered) = _ _ _ _ _ _
Average score for this section

Transfer your score to the transforming technology Index at the beginning of the Self-Assessment.

CRITERION #6: CONTROL:

INTENT: Implement the practical solution. Maintain the performance and correct possible complications.

In my belief, the answer to this question is clearly defined:

5 Strongly Agree

4 Agree

3 Neutral

2 Disagree

1 Strongly Disagree

1. What adjustments to the strategies are needed?
<--- Score

2. What other areas of the group might benefit from the transforming technology team's improvements, knowledge, and learning?
<--- Score

3. How will input, process, and output variables be

checked to detect for sub-optimal conditions?
<--- Score

4. Is a response plan in place for when the input, process, or output measures indicate an 'out-of-control' condition?
<--- Score

5. How will report readings be checked to effectively monitor performance?
<--- Score

6. How will new or emerging customer needs/requirements be checked/communicated to orient the process toward meeting the new specifications and continually reducing variation?
<--- Score

7. How do you monitor usage and cost?
<--- Score

8. Will any special training be provided for results interpretation?
<--- Score

9. How do you select, collect, align, and integrate transforming technology data and information for tracking daily operations and overall organizational performance, including progress relative to strategic objectives and action plans?
<--- Score

10. What is your theory of human motivation, and how does your compensation plan fit with that view?
<--- Score

11. Implementation Planning: is a pilot needed to test the changes before a full roll out occurs?
<--- Score

12. How do senior leaders actions reflect a commitment to the organizations transforming technology values?
<--- Score

13. What is the recommended frequency of auditing?
<--- Score

14. Have new or revised work instructions resulted?
<--- Score

15. What key inputs and outputs are being measured on an ongoing basis?
<--- Score

16. You may have created your quality measures at a time when you lacked resources, technology wasn't up to the required standard, or low service levels were the industry norm. Have those circumstances changed?
<--- Score

17. Can you adapt and adjust to changing transforming technology situations?
<--- Score

18. How do controls support value?
<--- Score

19. Is new knowledge gained imbedded in the response plan?
<--- Score

20. Are documented procedures clear and easy to follow for the operators?
<--- Score

21. What transforming technology standards are applicable?
<--- Score

22. Is there a standardized process?
<--- Score

23. Does the response plan contain a definite closed loop continual improvement scheme (e.g., plan-do-check-act)?
<--- Score

24. What should the next improvement project be that is related to transforming technology?
<--- Score

25. Who is the transforming technology process owner?
<--- Score

26. How widespread is its use?
<--- Score

27. What are the critical parameters to watch?
<--- Score

28. Will your goals reflect your program budget?
<--- Score

29. Is there a transforming technology Communication plan covering who needs to get what

information when?

<--- Score

30. How will the process owner verify improvement in present and future sigma levels, process capabilities?

<--- Score

31. Are new process steps, standards, and documentation ingrained into normal operations?

<--- Score

32. Can support from partners be adjusted?

<--- Score

33. How do you establish and deploy modified action plans if circumstances require a shift in plans and rapid execution of new plans?

<--- Score

34. Does job training on the documented procedures need to be part of the process team's education and training?

<--- Score

35. How do you spread information?

<--- Score

36. In the case of a transforming technology project, the criteria for the audit derive from implementation objectives, an audit of a transforming technology project involves assessing whether the recommendations outlined for implementation have been met, can you track that any transforming technology project is implemented as planned, and is it working?

<--- Score

37. Is a response plan established and deployed?
<--- Score

38. Has the improved process and its steps been standardized?
<--- Score

39. Is there a control plan in place for sustaining improvements (short and long-term)?
<--- Score

40. Who controls critical resources?
<--- Score

41. Act/Adjust: What Do you Need to Do Differently?
<--- Score

42. Do the transforming technology decisions you make today help people and the planet tomorrow?
<--- Score

43. Is knowledge gained on process shared and institutionalized?
<--- Score

44. How might the group capture best practices and lessons learned so as to leverage improvements?
<--- Score

45. How can you best use all of your knowledge repositories to enhance learning and sharing?
<--- Score

46. Are you measuring, monitoring and predicting transforming technology activities to optimize

operations and profitability, and enhancing outcomes?

<--- Score

47. Who is going to spread your message?

<--- Score

48. Is there documentation that will support the successful operation of the improvement?

<--- Score

49. How do you plan on providing proper recognition and disclosure of supporting companies?

<--- Score

50. Is there an action plan in case of emergencies?

<--- Score

51. How do you plan for the cost of succession?

<--- Score

52. What should you measure to verify efficiency gains?

<--- Score

53. What do your reports reflect?

<--- Score

54. Does the transforming technology performance meet the customer's requirements?

<--- Score

55. How do you encourage people to take control and responsibility?

<--- Score

56. Will existing staff require re-training, for example, to learn new business processes?
<--- Score

57. What are the key elements of your transforming technology performance improvement system, including your evaluation, organizational learning, and innovation processes?
<--- Score

58. Is there a transfer of ownership and knowledge to process owner and process team tasked with the responsibilities.
<--- Score

59. What quality tools were useful in the control phase?
<--- Score

60. Are there documented procedures?
<--- Score

61. What is the control/monitoring plan?
<--- Score

62. How is transforming technology project cost planned, managed, monitored?
<--- Score

63. What is your plan to assess your security risks?
<--- Score

64. Does transforming technology appropriately measure and monitor risk?
<--- Score

65. Is the transforming technology test/monitoring cost justified?
<--- Score

66. Who will be in control?
<--- Score

67. Where do ideas that reach policy makers and planners as proposals for transforming technology strengthening and reform actually originate?
<--- Score

68. Has the transforming technology value of standards been quantified?
<--- Score

69. Are the planned controls in place?
<--- Score

70. What can you control?
<--- Score

71. How will you measure your QA plan's effectiveness?
<--- Score

72. Do you monitor the effectiveness of your transforming technology activities?
<--- Score

73. Are pertinent alerts monitored, analyzed and distributed to appropriate personnel?
<--- Score

74. What other systems, operations, processes, and

infrastructures (hiring practices, staffing, training, incentives/rewards, metrics/dashboards/scorecards, etc.) need updates, additions, changes, or deletions in order to facilitate knowledge transfer and improvements?
<--- Score

75. Are suggested corrective/restorative actions indicated on the response plan for known causes to problems that might surface?
<--- Score

76. Is there a recommended audit plan for routine surveillance inspections of transforming technology's gains?
<--- Score

77. Are operating procedures consistent?
<--- Score

78. Are the transforming technology standards challenging?
<--- Score

79. What do you stand for--and what are you against?
<--- Score

80. How is change control managed?
<--- Score

81. Will the team be available to assist members in planning investigations?
<--- Score

82. How will the day-to-day responsibilities for monitoring and continual improvement be

transferred from the improvement team to the process owner?
<--- Score

83. Does a troubleshooting guide exist or is it needed?
<--- Score

84. What are you attempting to measure/monitor?
<--- Score

85. Is there a documented and implemented monitoring plan?
<--- Score

86. Is reporting being used or needed?
<--- Score

87. How will the process owner and team be able to hold the gains?
<--- Score

88. Do you monitor the transforming technology decisions made and fine tune them as they evolve?
<--- Score

89. Are the planned controls working?
<--- Score

90. What do you measure to verify effectiveness gains?
<--- Score

91. What is the standard for acceptable transforming technology performance?
<--- Score

92. What are the known security controls?
<--- Score

93. How do your controls stack up?
<--- Score

Add up total points for this section:
_____ = Total points for this section

Divided by: _____ (number of
statements answered) = _____
Average score for this section

Transfer your score to the transforming
technology Index at the beginning of
the Self-Assessment.

CRITERION #7: SUSTAIN:

INTENT: Retain the benefits.

In my belief, the answer to this question is clearly defined:

5 Strongly Agree

4 Agree

3 Neutral

2 Disagree

1 Strongly Disagree

1. What management system can you use to leverage the transforming technology experience, ideas, and concerns of the people closest to the work to be done?
<--- Score

2. Are the criteria for selecting recommendations stated?
<--- Score

3. How important is transforming technology to the

user organizations mission?
<--- Score

4. What is the estimated value of the project?
<--- Score

5. What are the long-term transforming technology goals?
<--- Score

6. Who will provide the final approval of transforming technology deliverables?
<--- Score

7. What trophy do you want on your mantle?
<--- Score

8. What is the range of capabilities?
<--- Score

9. Is a transforming technology team work effort in place?
<--- Score

10. What should you stop doing?
<--- Score

11. What are specific transforming technology rules to follow?
<--- Score

12. Who have you, as a company, historically been when you've been at your best?
<--- Score

13. Is there a work around that you can use?

<--- Score

14. How is implementation research currently incorporated into each of your goals?
<--- Score

15. What are the top 3 things at the forefront of your transforming technology agendas for the next 3 years?
<--- Score

16. If you do not follow, then how to lead?
<--- Score

17. What is effective transforming technology?
<--- Score

18. Is it economical; do you have the time and money?
<--- Score

19. Do you feel that more should be done in the transforming technology area?
<--- Score

20. Do you have enough freaky customers in your portfolio pushing you to the limit day in and day out?
<--- Score

21. Why will customers want to buy your organizations products/services?
<--- Score

22. What have been your experiences in defining long range transforming technology goals?
<--- Score

23. At what moment would you think; Will I get fired?
<--- Score

24. What are the performance and scale of the transforming technology tools?
<--- Score

25. Is there any existing transforming technology governance structure?
<--- Score

26. How do you keep records, of what?
<--- Score

27. How do you track customer value, profitability or financial return, organizational success, and sustainability?
<--- Score

28. If there were zero limitations, what would you do differently?
<--- Score

29. What are the success criteria that will indicate that transforming technology objectives have been met and the benefits delivered?
<--- Score

30. What happens if you do not have enough funding?
<--- Score

31. Who will determine interim and final deadlines?
<--- Score

32. Who, on the executive team or the board, has spoken to a customer recently?
<--- Score

33. What is the source of the strategies for transforming technology strengthening and reform?
<--- Score

34. How do customers see your organization?
<--- Score

35. Who is responsible for ensuring appropriate resources (time, people and money) are allocated to transforming technology?
<--- Score

36. What is the kind of project structure that would be appropriate for your transforming technology project, should it be formal and complex, or can it be less formal and relatively simple?
<--- Score

37. How can you become more high-tech but still be high touch?
<--- Score

38. What are you challenging?
<--- Score

39. Whom among your colleagues do you trust, and for what?
<--- Score

40. What is the overall talent health of your organization as a whole at senior levels, and for

each organization reporting to a member of the Senior Leadership Team?
<--- Score

41. What would have to be true for the option on the table to be the best possible choice?
<--- Score

42. How do you lead with transforming technology in mind?
<--- Score

43. Do you think transforming technology accomplishes the goals you expect it to accomplish?
<--- Score

44. What is your competitive advantage?
<--- Score

45. What new services of functionality will be implemented next with transforming technology ?
<--- Score

46. How can you negotiate transforming technology successfully with a stubborn boss, an irate client, or a deceitful coworker?
<--- Score

47. Ask yourself: how would you do this work if you only had one staff member to do it?
<--- Score

48. Are you / should you be revolutionary or evolutionary?
<--- Score

49. What is the overall business strategy?
<--- Score

50. How do you maintain transforming technology's Integrity?
<--- Score

51. Is the impact that transforming technology has shown?
<--- Score

52. What trouble can you get into?
<--- Score

53. Operational - will it work?
<--- Score

54. What is it like to work for you?
<--- Score

55. What are current transforming technology paradigms?
<--- Score

56. Where can you break convention?
<--- Score

57. Have benefits been optimized with all key stakeholders?
<--- Score

58. In retrospect, of the projects that you pulled the plug on, what percent do you wish had been allowed to keep going, and what percent do you wish had ended earlier?
<--- Score

59. Are there any activities that you can take off your to do list?
<--- Score

60. Who do you want your customers to become?
<--- Score

61. Why do and why don't your customers like your organization?
<--- Score

62. Do you have past transforming technology successes?
<--- Score

63. What unique value proposition (UVP) do you offer?
<--- Score

64. What are you trying to prove to yourself, and how might it be hijacking your life and business success?
<--- Score

65. What one word do you want to own in the minds of your customers, employees, and partners?
<--- Score

66. Has implementation been effective in reaching specified objectives so far?
<--- Score

67. How do you ensure that implementations of transforming technology products are done in a way that ensures safety?
<--- Score

68. If you got fired and a new hire took your place, what would she do different?
<--- Score

69. How do you create buy-in?
<--- Score

70. What would you recommend your friend do if he/she were facing this dilemma?
<--- Score

71. What role does communication play in the success or failure of a transforming technology project?
<--- Score

72. Instead of going to current contacts for new ideas, what if you reconnected with dormant contacts-- the people you used to know? If you were going reactivate a dormant tie, who would it be?
<--- Score

73. Can you break it down?
<--- Score

74. What are the short and long-term transforming technology goals?
<--- Score

75. How do you provide a safe environment -physically and emotionally?
<--- Score

76. Who are your customers?
<--- Score

77. What is the big transforming technology idea?
<--- Score

78. Who will manage the integration of tools?
<--- Score

79. Who is the main stakeholder, with ultimate responsibility for driving transforming technology forward?
<--- Score

80. Do you think you know, or do you know you know ?
<--- Score

81. What counts that you are not counting?
<--- Score

82. Political -is anyone trying to undermine this project?
<--- Score

83. How do you manage transforming technology Knowledge Management (KM)?
<--- Score

84. Are you changing as fast as the world around you?
<--- Score

85. What is an unauthorized commitment?
<--- Score

86. How will you motivate the stakeholders with the least vested interest?
<--- Score

87. What threat is transforming technology addressing?

<--- Score

88. Are you using a design thinking approach and integrating Innovation, transforming technology Experience, and Brand Value?

<--- Score

89. Did your employees make progress today?

<--- Score

90. What projects are going on in the organization today, and what resources are those projects using from the resource pools?

<--- Score

91. What are the usability implications of transforming technology actions?

<--- Score

92. How will you insure seamless interoperability of transforming technology moving forward?

<--- Score

93. What business benefits will transforming technology goals deliver if achieved?

<--- Score

94. What is the craziest thing you can do?

<--- Score

95. What are your personal philosophies regarding transforming technology and how do they influence your work?

<--- Score

96. How does transforming technology integrate with other stakeholder initiatives?
<--- Score

97. What are the key enablers to make this transforming technology move?
<--- Score

98. What you are going to do to affect the numbers?
<--- Score

99. How can you become the company that would put you out of business?
<--- Score

100. How do you govern and fulfill your societal responsibilities?
<--- Score

101. What does your signature ensure?
<--- Score

102. Whose voice (department, ethnic group, women, older workers, etc) might you have missed hearing from in your company, and how might you amplify this voice to create positive momentum for your business?
<--- Score

103. Are new benefits received and understood?
<--- Score

104. What could happen if you do not do it?

<--- Score

105. Which transforming technology goals are the most important?
<--- Score

106. What is your question? Why?
<--- Score

107. Do you have the right capabilities and capacities?
<--- Score

108. How do you cross-sell and up-sell your transforming technology success?
<--- Score

109. What may be the consequences for the performance of an organization if all stakeholders are not consulted regarding transforming technology?
<--- Score

110. Can you do all this work?
<--- Score

111. How will you ensure you get what you expected?
<--- Score

112. Are all key stakeholders present at all Structured Walkthroughs?
<--- Score

113. Who is responsible for transforming technology?
<--- Score

114. Marketing budgets are tighter, consumers are more skeptical, and social media has changed forever the way we talk about transforming technology, how do you gain traction?
<--- Score

115. If you had to leave your organization for a year and the only communication you could have with employees/colleagues was a single paragraph, what would you write?
<--- Score

116. Do you have an implicit bias for capital investments over people investments?
<--- Score

117. What is your BATNA (best alternative to a negotiated agreement)?
<--- Score

118. When information truly is ubiquitous, when reach and connectivity are completely global, when computing resources are infinite, and when a whole new set of impossibilities are not only possible, but happening, what will that do to your business?
<--- Score

119. What are your most important goals for the strategic transforming technology objectives?
<--- Score

120. Have new benefits been realized?
<--- Score

121. How do you determine the key elements that

affect transforming technology workforce satisfaction, how are these elements determined for different workforce groups and segments?
<--- Score

122. What are the rules and assumptions your industry operates under? What if the opposite were true?
<--- Score

123. How can you incorporate support to ensure safe and effective use of transforming technology into the services that you provide?
<--- Score

124. If you weren't already in this business, would you enter it today? And if not, what are you going to do about it?
<--- Score

125. Who are the key stakeholders?
<--- Score

126. Is transforming technology realistic, or are you setting yourself up for failure?
<--- Score

127. How much contingency will be available in the budget?
<--- Score

128. What potential megatrends could make your business model obsolete?
<--- Score

129. How do you accomplish your long range transforming technology goals?

<--- Score

130. Do you know who is a friend or a foe?
<--- Score

131. How do you transition from the baseline to the target?
<--- Score

132. Who are four people whose careers you have enhanced?
<--- Score

133. Is the transforming technology organization completing tasks effectively and efficiently?
<--- Score

134. Are the assumptions believable and achievable?
<--- Score

135. Is transforming technology dependent on the successful delivery of a current project?
<--- Score

136. How are you doing compared to your industry?
<--- Score

137. What stupid rule would you most like to kill?
<--- Score

138. What are the business goals transforming technology is aiming to achieve?
<--- Score

139. Who will be responsible for deciding whether

transforming technology goes ahead or not after the initial investigations?

<--- Score

140. What happens when a new employee joins the organization?

<--- Score

141. What are internal and external transforming technology relations?

<--- Score

142. If no one would ever find out about your accomplishments, how would you lead differently?

<--- Score

143. What do we do when new problems arise?

<--- Score

144. Why not do transforming technology?

<--- Score

145. What happens at your organization when people fail?

<--- Score

146. Do transforming technology rules make a reasonable demand on a users capabilities?

<--- Score

147. What are the barriers to increased transforming technology production?

<--- Score

148. Think of your transforming technology project, what are the main functions?

<--- Score

149. How do you know if you are successful?
<--- Score

150. How do you stay inspired?
<--- Score

151. What are the potential basics of transforming technology fraud?
<--- Score

152. How do you proactively clarify deliverables and transforming technology quality expectations?
<--- Score

153. Are you satisfied with your current role? If not, what is missing from it?
<--- Score

154. Are assumptions made in transforming technology stated explicitly?
<--- Score

155. How do you keep the momentum going?
<--- Score

156. Is there any reason to believe the opposite of my current belief?
<--- Score

157. If your company went out of business tomorrow, would anyone who doesn't get a paycheck here care?
<--- Score

158. How do you set transforming technology stretch targets and how do you get people to not only participate in setting these stretch targets but also that they strive to achieve these?
<--- Score

159. Would you rather sell to knowledgeable and informed customers or to uninformed customers?
<--- Score

160. Why is transforming technology important for you now?
<--- Score

161. Do you have the right people on the bus?
<--- Score

162. How much does transforming technology help?
<--- Score

163. What is the funding source for this project?
<--- Score

164. Is a transforming technology breakthrough on the horizon?
<--- Score

165. Are you making progress, and are you making progress as transforming technology leaders?
<--- Score

166. Who is responsible for errors?
<--- Score

167. What was the last experiment you ran?

<--- Score

168. Which models, tools and techniques are necessary?
<--- Score

169. What is your transforming technology strategy?
<--- Score

170. What will be the consequences to the stakeholder (financial, reputation etc) if transforming technology does not go ahead or fails to deliver the objectives?
<--- Score

171. Will it be accepted by users?
<--- Score

172. Why should people listen to you?
<--- Score

173. How do you assess the transforming technology pitfalls that are inherent in implementing it?
<--- Score

174. If you had to rebuild your organization without any traditional competitive advantages (i.e., no killer technology, promising research, innovative product/ service delivery model, etcetera), how would your people have to approach their work and collaborate together in order to create the necessary conditions for success?
<--- Score

175. Is your basic point _____ or _____?
<--- Score

176. In the past year, what have you done (or could you have done) to increase the accurate perception of your company/brand as ethical and honest?

<--- Score

177. How do you foster the skills, knowledge, talents, attributes, and characteristics you want to have?

<--- Score

178. What goals did you miss?

<--- Score

179. Who else should you help?

<--- Score

180. Can you maintain your growth without detracting from the factors that have contributed to your success?

<--- Score

181. In a project to restructure transforming technology outcomes, which stakeholders would you involve?

<--- Score

182. What are strategies for increasing support and reducing opposition?

<--- Score

183. What is the purpose of transforming technology in relation to the mission?

<--- Score

184. What information is critical to your organization

that your executives are ignoring?
<--- Score

185. If your customer were your grandmother, would you tell her to buy what you're selling?
<--- Score

186. Is your strategy driving your strategy? Or is the way in which you allocate resources driving your strategy?
<--- Score

187. How do you engage the workforce, in addition to satisfying them?
<--- Score

188. How do you make it meaningful in connecting transforming technology with what users do day-to-day?
<--- Score

189. How do you listen to customers to obtain actionable information?
<--- Score

190. What is the recommended frequency of auditing?
<--- Score

191. What are the essentials of internal transforming technology management?
<--- Score

192. Is maximizing transforming technology protection the same as minimizing transforming technology loss?

<--- Score

193. What knowledge, skills and characteristics mark a good transforming technology project manager?
<--- Score

194. How do you go about securing transforming technology?
<--- Score

195. Do you see more potential in people than they do in themselves?
<--- Score

196. How do you deal with transforming technology changes?
<--- Score

197. To whom do you add value?
<--- Score

198. Are your responses positive or negative?
<--- Score

199. Why is it important to have senior management support for a transforming technology project?
<--- Score

200. Who is on the team?
<--- Score

201. Do you say no to customers for no reason?
<--- Score

202. How will you know that the transforming

technology project has been successful?
<--- Score

203. Who uses your product in ways you never expected?
<--- Score

204. Will there be any necessary staff changes (redundancies or new hires)?
<--- Score

205. Were lessons learned captured and communicated?
<--- Score

206. Are you paying enough attention to the partners your company depends on to succeed?
<--- Score

207. What is something you believe that nearly no one agrees with you on?
<--- Score

208. Who do we want your customers to become?
<--- Score

209. What are the gaps in your knowledge and experience?
<--- Score

Add up total points for this section:
_ _ _ _ _ = Total points for this section

Divided by: _ _ _ _ _ _ (number of statements answered) = _ _ _ _ _ _
Average score for this section

Transfer your score to the transforming
technology Index at the beginning of
the Self-Assessment.

Transforming Technology and Managing Projects, Criteria for Project Managers:

1.0 Initiating Process Group: Transforming Technology

1. What will be the pressing issues of tomorrow?

2. Do you know all the stakeholders impacted by the Transforming Technology project and what needs are?

3. What were things that you need to improve?

4. Does it make any difference if you am successful?

5. How is each deliverable reviewed, verified, and validated?

6. What are the pressing issues of the hour?

7. Who is involved in each phase?

8. Were resources available as planned?

9. What are the short and long term implications?

10. Were escalated issues resolved promptly?

11. What are the constraints?

12. How will you know you did it?

13. If action is called for, what form should it take?

14. Do you know the roles & responsibilities required for this Transforming Technology project?

15. At which stage, in a typical Transforming

Technology project do stake holders have maximum influence?

16. Information sharing?

17. Have you evaluated the teams performance and asked for feedback?

18. If the risk event occurs, what will you do?

19. Which six sigma dmaic phase focuses on why and how defects and errors occur?

20. How can you make your needs known?

1.1 Project Charter: Transforming Technology

21. Assumptions and constraints: what assumptions were made in defining the Transforming Technology project?

22. When?

23. What ideas do you have for initial tests of change (PDSA cycles)?

24. Are you building in-house ?

25. Environmental stewardship and sustainability considerations: what is the process that will be used to ensure compliance with the environmental stewardship policy?

26. Fit with other Products Compliments – Cannibalizes?

27. What does it need to do?

28. Customer: who are you doing the Transforming Technology project for?

29. Why Outsource?

30. Where and how does the team fit within your organization structure?

31. What metrics could you look at?

32. What is the purpose of the Transforming Technology project?

33. Is time of the essence?

34. Run it as as a startup?

35. Avoid costs, improve service, and/ or comply with a mandate?

36. What goes into your Transforming Technology project Charter?

37. Does the Transforming Technology project need to consider any special capacity or capability issues?

38. What changes can you make to improve?

39. What is the business need?

40. Pop quiz – which are the same inputs as in the Transforming Technology project charter?

1.2 Stakeholder Register: Transforming Technology

41. Who is managing stakeholder engagement?

42. How will reports be created?

43. What & Why?

44. What are the major Transforming Technology project milestones requiring communications or providing communications opportunities?

45. How much influence do they have on the Transforming Technology project?

46. Who wants to talk about Security?

47. Who are the stakeholders?

48. How should employers make voices heard?

49. How big is the gap?

50. What opportunities exist to provide communications?

51. What is the power of the stakeholder?

52. Is your organization ready for change?

1.3 Stakeholder Analysis Matrix: Transforming Technology

53. Partnerships, agencies, distribution?

54. How do you manage Transforming Technology project Risk?

55. What is relationship with the Transforming Technology project?

56. Economy - home, abroad?

57. Is there a reason why you are or are not not using an external rating system?

58. Arena: in what fields are the actors active, where are they present?

59. New technologies, services, ideas?

60. Volumes, production, economies?

61. How to measure the achievement of the Immediate Objective?

62. What do your organizations stakeholders do better than anyone else?

63. Who determines value?

64. How to measure the achievement of the Development Objective?

65. Political effects?

66. Does your organization have bad debt or cash-flow problems?

67. Gaps in capabilities?

68. How does the Transforming Technology project involve consultations or collaboration with other organizations?

69. Sustaining internal capabilities?

70. What is the relationship among stakeholders?

71. Do any safeguard policies apply to the Transforming Technology project?

72. Partnership opportunities/synergies?

2.0 Planning Process Group: Transforming Technology

73. In what ways can the governance of the Transforming Technology project be improved so that it has greater likelihood of achieving future sustainability?

74. If you are late, will anybody notice?

75. How will users learn how to use the deliverables?

76. Who are the Transforming Technology project stakeholders?

77. Is the pace of implementing the products of the program ensuring the completeness of the results of the Transforming Technology project?

78. How does activity resource estimation affect activity duration estimation?

79. The Transforming Technology project charter is created in which Transforming Technology project management process group?

80. What should you do next?

81. Did the program design/ implementation strategy adequately address the planning stage necessary to set up structures, hire staff etc.?

82. If task x starts two days late, what is the effect on

the Transforming Technology project end date?

83. Does it make any difference if you are successful?

84. How will it affect you?

85. To what extent have public/private national resources and/or counterparts been mobilized to contribute to the programs objective and produce results and impacts?

86. What is involved in Transforming Technology project scope management, and why is good Transforming Technology project scope management so important on information technology Transforming Technology projects?

87. How well defined and documented are the Transforming Technology project management processes you chose to use?

88. You are creating your WBS and find that you keep decomposing tasks into smaller and smaller units. How can you tell when you are done?

89. What do you need to do?

90. Did you read it correctly?

91. On which process should team members spend the most time?

92. What good practices or successful experiences or transferable examples have been identified?

2.1 Project Management Plan: Transforming Technology

93. Is the budget realistic?

94. Is the engineering content at a feasibility level-of-detail, and is it sufficiently complete, to provide an adequate basis for the baseline cost estimate?

95. Are there non-structural buyout or relocation recommendations?

96. What are the training needs?

97. Is the appropriate plan selected based on your organizations objectives and evaluation criteria expressed in Principles and Guidelines policies?

98. What data/reports/tools/etc. do your PMs need?

99. Why Change?

100. Are comparable cost estimates used for comparing, screening and selecting alternative plans, and has a reasonable cost estimate been developed for the recommended plan?

101. When is the Transforming Technology project management plan created?

102. If the Transforming Technology project management plan is a comprehensive document that guides you in Transforming Technology project

execution and control, then what should it NOT contain?

103. What are the deliverables?

104. If the Transforming Technology project is complex or scope is specialized, do you have appropriate and/or qualified staff available to perform the tasks?

105. What are the assigned resources?

106. Do there need to be organizational changes?

107. Who manages integration?

108. How do you organize the costs in the Transforming Technology project management plan?

109. Who is the sponsor?

110. What is the justification?

111. When is a Transforming Technology project management plan created?

2.2 Scope Management Plan: Transforming Technology

112. Has your organization done similar tasks before?

113. Have the key elements of a coherent Transforming Technology project management strategy been established?

114. Are adequate resources provided for the quality assurance function?

115. During what part of the PM process is the Transforming Technology project scope statement created?

116. Have Transforming Technology project management standards and procedures been identified / established and documented?

117. Will the Transforming Technology project deliverables become accepted in writing?

118. Are staff skills known and available for each task?

119. Is there a requirements change management processes in place?

120. Has a quality assurance plan been developed for the Transforming Technology project?

121. Have the scope, objectives, costs, benefits and impacts been communicated to all involved and/or

impacted stakeholders and work groups?

122. How do you handle uncertainty or conflict?

123. Are post milestone Transforming Technology project reviews (PMPR) conducted with your organization at least once a year?

124. Are the quality tools and methods identified in the Quality Plan appropriate to the Transforming Technology project?

125. Are funding resource estimates sufficiently detailed and documented for use in planning and tracking the Transforming Technology project?

126. When is corrective or preventative action required?

127. Is there a Transforming Technology project organization chart showing the reporting relationships and responsibilities for each position?

128. Does the resource management plan include a personnel development plan?

129. Has a resource management plan been created?

130. Have the key functions and capabilities been defined and assigned to each release or iteration?

131. Are target dates established for each milestone deliverable?

2.3 Requirements Management Plan: Transforming Technology

132. What is a problem?

133. Is it new or replacing an existing business system or process?

134. Should you include sub-activities?

135. Who will finally present the work or product(s) for acceptance?

136. How will bidders price evaluations be done, by deliverables, phases, or in a big bang?

137. Did you use declarative statements?

138. What went right?

139. Is any organizational data being used or stored?

140. Who is responsible for quantifying the Transforming Technology project requirements?

141. How detailed should the Transforming Technology project get?

142. After the requirements are gathered and set forth on the requirements register, theyre little more than a laundry list of items. Some may be duplicates, some might conflict with others and some will be too broad or too vague to understand. Describe how the

requirements will be analyzed. Who will perform the analysis?

143. To see if a requirement statement is sufficiently well-defined, read it from the developers perspective. Mentally add the phrase, call me when youre done to the end of the requirement and see if that makes you nervous. In other words, would you need additional clarification from the author to understand the requirement well enough to design and implement it?

144. Is the system software (non-operating system) new to the IT Transforming Technology project team?

145. What are you counting on?

146. Will the contractors involved take full responsibility?

147. Have stakeholders been instructed in the Change Control process?

148. Do you have an appropriate arrangement for meetings?

149. What information regarding the Transforming Technology project requirements will be reported?

150. Do you know which stakeholders will participate in the requirements effort?

151. Will you document changes to requirements?

2.4 Requirements Documentation: Transforming Technology

152. What will be the integration problems?

153. What images does it conjure?

154. Does your organization restrict technical alternatives?

155. Is the requirement realistically testable?

156. What are current process problems?

157. How linear / iterative is your Requirements Gathering process (or will it be)?

158. How do you get the user to tell you what they want?

159. How much does requirements engineering cost?

160. Verifiability. can the requirements be checked?

161. What is a show stopper in the requirements?

162. Is the origin of the requirement clearly stated?

163. How can you document system requirements?

164. What can tools do for us?

165. How much testing do you need to do to prove

that your system is safe?

166. What is your Elevator Speech?

167. Does the system provide the functions which best support the customers needs?

168. The problem with gathering requirements is right there in the word gathering. What images does it conjure?

169. Can you check system requirements?

170. Have the benefits identified with the system being identified clearly?

171. What variations exist for a process?

2.5 Requirements Traceability Matrix: Transforming Technology

172. What percentage of Transforming Technology projects are producing traceability matrices between requirements and other work products?

173. What is the WBS?

174. Is there a requirements traceability process in place?

175. What are the chronologies, contingencies, consequences, criteria?

176. Will you use a Requirements Traceability Matrix?

177. How small is small enough?

178. Describe the process for approving requirements so they can be added to the traceability matrix and Transforming Technology project work can be performed. Will the Transforming Technology project requirements become approved in writing?

179. Why use a WBS?

180. How do you manage scope?

181. Do you have a clear understanding of all subcontracts in place?

182. Why do you manage scope?

183. How will it affect the stakeholders personally in career?

2.6 Project Scope Statement: Transforming Technology

184. Will all tasks resulting from issues be entered into the Transforming Technology project Plan and tracked through the plan?

185. Are the input requirements from the team members clearly documented and communicated?

186. Will statistics related to QA be collected, trends analyzed, and problems raised as issues?

187. Will the Transforming Technology project risks be managed according to the Transforming Technology projects risk management process?

188. Was planning completed before the Transforming Technology project was initiated?

189. Elements of scope management that deal with concept development ?

190. Has the format for tracking and monitoring schedules and costs been defined?

191. Risks?

192. Once its defined, what is the stability of the Transforming Technology project scope?

193. Will you need a statement of work?

194. Is the quality function identified and assigned?

195. If the scope changes, what will the impact be to your Transforming Technology project in terms of duration, cost, quality, or any other important areas of the Transforming Technology project?

196. Is the change control process documented and on file?

197. Identify how your team and you will create the Transforming Technology project scope statement and the work breakdown structure (WBS). Document how you will create the Transforming Technology project scope statement and WBS, and make sure you answer the following questions: In defining Transforming Technology project scope and the WBS, will you and your Transforming Technology project team be using methods defined by your organization, methods defined by the Transforming Technology project management office (PMO), or other methods?

198. Is the plan under configuration management?

199. Relevant - ask yourself can you get there; why are you doing this Transforming Technology project?

200. If there are vendors, have they signed off on the Transforming Technology project Plan?

201. What is change?

202. Do you anticipate new stakeholders joining the Transforming Technology project over time?

2.7 Assumption and Constraint Log: Transforming Technology

203. Are processes for release management of new development from coding and unit testing, to integration testing, to training, and production defined and followed?

204. Can you perform this task or activity in a more effective manner?

205. Does a documented Transforming Technology project organizational policy & plan (i.e. governance model) exist?

206. Would known impacts serve as impediments?

207. What if failure during recovery?

208. What worked well?

209. Contradictory information between document sections?

210. What strengths do you have?

211. Is the amount of effort justified by the anticipated value of forming a new process?

212. What other teams / processes would be impacted by changes to the current process, and how?

213. How many Transforming Technology project staff

does this specific process affect?

214. Have all necessary approvals been obtained?

215. How relevant is this attribute to this Transforming Technology project or audit?

216. What threats might prevent you from getting there?

217. How are new requirements or changes to requirements identified?

218. Is there a Steering Committee in place?

219. Has a Transforming Technology project Communications Plan been developed?

220. Does the document/deliverable meet general requirements (for example, statement of work) for all deliverables?

221. Contradictory information between different documents?

2.8 Work Breakdown Structure: Transforming Technology

222. When do you stop?

223. When would you develop a Work Breakdown Structure?

224. Why is it useful?

225. Do you need another level?

226. How many levels?

227. Where does it take place?

228. What is the probability of completing the Transforming Technology project in less that xx days?

229. How much detail?

230. Is the work breakdown structure (wbs) defined and is the scope of the Transforming Technology project clear with assigned deliverable owners?

231. When does it have to be done?

232. Can you make it?

233. What is the probability that the Transforming Technology project duration will exceed xx weeks?

234. Is it still viable?

235. What has to be done?

236. Who has to do it?

237. How big is a work-package?

238. How will you and your Transforming Technology project team define the Transforming Technology projects scope and work breakdown structure?

2.9 WBS Dictionary: Transforming Technology

239. Incurrence of actual indirect costs in excess of budgets, by element of expense?

240. Budgets assigned to control accounts?

241. What is the end result of a work package?

242. Time-phased control account budgets?

243. Knowledgeable Transforming Technology projections of future performance?

244. Is subcontracted work defined and identified to the appropriate subcontractor within the proper WBS element?

245. Should you have a test for each code module?

246. Are Transforming Technology projected overhead costs in each pool and the associated direct costs used as the basis for establishing interim rates for allocating overhead to contracts?

247. Are work packages reasonably short in time duration or do they have adequate objective indicators/milestones to minimize subjectivity of the in process work evaluation?

248. Is all budget available as management reserve identified and excluded from the performance

measurement baseline?

249. Are the variances between budgeted and actual indirect costs identified and analyzed at the level of assigned responsibility for control (indirect pool, department, etc.)?

250. Is the work done on a work package level as described in the WBS dictionary?

251. Are overhead costs budgets established on a basis consistent with anticipated direct business base?

252. Major functional areas of contract effort?

253. Does the contractors system include procedures for measuring performance of the lowest level organization responsible for the control account?

254. Is cost and schedule performance measurement done in a consistent, systematic manner?

255. Are authorized changes being incorporated in a timely manner?

256. Are current budgets resulting from changes to the authorized work and/or internal replanning, reconcilable to original budgets for specified reporting items?

257. Is the anticipated (firm and potential) business base Transforming Technology projected in a rational, consistent manner?

2.10 Schedule Management Plan: Transforming Technology

258. Is there a set of procedures defining the scope, procedures, and deliverables defining quality control?

259. Are the payment terms being followed?

260. Alignment to strategic goals & objectives?

261. Is the ims development and management approach described?

262. Are the people assigned to the Transforming Technology project sufficiently qualified?

263. Are the schedule estimates reasonable given the Transforming Technology project?

264. How relevant is this attribute to this Transforming Technology project or audit?

265. Timeline and milestones?

266. Is the schedule feasible and at what cost?

267. Does the time Transforming Technology projection include an amount for contingencies (time reserves)?

268. Has a sponsor been identified?

269. What date will the task finish?

270. Are the appropriate IT resources adequate to meet planned commitments?

271. Will the tools selected accomplish the scheduling needs?

272. Are vendor invoices audited for accuracy before payment?

273. Are the activity durations realistic and at an appropriate level of detail for effective management?

274. Are all payments made according to the contract(s)?

275. Does the Transforming Technology project have a formal Transforming Technology project Charter?

276. Are actuals compared against estimates to analyze and correct variances?

277. What does a valid Schedule look like?

2.11 Activity List: Transforming Technology

278. What will be performed?

279. When will the work be performed?

280. How do you determine the late start (LS) for each activity?

281. When do the individual activities need to start and finish?

282. What is the total time required to complete the Transforming Technology project if no delays occur?

283. What is the LF and LS for each activity?

284. How much slack is available in the Transforming Technology project?

285. How difficult will it be to do specific activities on this Transforming Technology project?

286. In what sequence?

287. Who will perform the work?

288. For other activities, how much delay can be tolerated?

289. What went well?

290. What is the probability the Transforming Technology project can be completed in xx weeks?

291. How can the Transforming Technology project be displayed graphically to better visualize the activities?

292. Where will it be performed?

293. How should ongoing costs be monitored to try to keep the Transforming Technology project within budget?

294. What is your organizations history in doing similar activities?

295. How will it be performed?

2.12 Activity Attributes: Transforming Technology

296. How many days do you need to complete the work scope with a limit of X number of resources?

297. How difficult will it be to complete specific activities on this Transforming Technology project?

298. Time for overtime?

299. Does your organization of the data change its meaning?

300. Which method produces the more accurate cost assignment?

301. Can more resources be added?

302. How do you manage time?

303. What conclusions/generalizations can you draw from this?

304. Activity: what is Missing?

305. What is missing?

306. Has management defined a definite timeframe for the turnaround or Transforming Technology project window?

307. Is there anything planned that does not need to

be here?

308. Activity: what is In the Bag?

309. Do you feel very comfortable with your prediction?

310. What went wrong?

311. Have constraints been applied to the start and finish milestones for the phases?

312. How many resources do you need to complete the work scope within a limit of X number of days?

313. What is the general pattern here?

314. Have you identified the Activity Leveling Priority code value on each activity?

2.13 Milestone List: Transforming Technology

315. Describe your organizations strengths and core competencies. What factors will make your organization succeed?

316. Competitive advantages?

317. How soon can the activity start?

318. Describe the industry you are in and the market growth opportunities. What is the market for your technology, product or service?

319. What are your competitors vulnerabilities?

320. Marketing - reach, distribution, awareness?

321. Which path is the critical path?

322. Environmental effects?

323. Who will manage the Transforming Technology project on a day-to-day basis?

324. New USPs?

325. How will the milestone be verified?

326. Loss of key staff?

327. Level of the Innovation?

328. Effects on core activities, distraction?

329. Usps (unique selling points)?

2.14 Network Diagram: Transforming Technology

330. What are the Key Success Factors?

331. Which type of network diagram allows you to depict four types of dependencies?

332. If the Transforming Technology project network diagram cannot change and you have extra personnel resources, what is the BEST thing to do?

333. What job or jobs precede it?

334. What is the lowest cost to complete this Transforming Technology project in xx weeks?

335. What controls the start and finish of a job?

336. What job or jobs could run concurrently?

337. What job or jobs follow it?

338. What is the completion time?

339. Where do you schedule uncertainty time?

340. If x is long, what would be the completion time if you break x into two parallel parts of y weeks and z weeks?

341. Are you on time?

342. What must be completed before an activity can be started?

343. What activity must be completed immediately before this activity can start?

344. Review the logical flow of the network diagram. Take a look at which activities you have first and then sequence the activities. Do they make sense?

345. What is the probability of completing the Transforming Technology project in less that xx days?

346. What are the Major Administrative Issues?

2.15 Activity Resource Requirements: Transforming Technology

347. When does monitoring begin?

348. How many signatures do you require on a check and does this match what is in your policy and procedures?

349. What is the Work Plan Standard?

350. Other support in specific areas?

351. What are constraints that you might find during the Human Resource Planning process?

352. Which logical relationship does the PDM use most often?

353. Why do you do that?

354. Do you use tools like decomposition and rolling-wave planning to produce the activity list and other outputs?

355. How do you handle petty cash?

356. Anything else?

357. Organizational Applicability?

358. Are there unresolved issues that need to be addressed?

2.16 Resource Breakdown Structure: Transforming Technology

359. What defines a successful Transforming Technology project?

360. Goals for the Transforming Technology project. What is each stakeholders desired outcome for the Transforming Technology project?

361. What can you do to improve productivity?

362. Why time management?

363. How should the information be delivered?

364. Which resource planning tool provides information on resource responsibility and accountability?

365. What is Transforming Technology project communication management?

366. What is the number one predictor of a groups productivity?

367. Which resources should be in the resource pool?

368. Why do you do it?

369. Who will be used as a Transforming Technology project team member?

370. Is predictive resource analysis being done?

371. What is each stakeholders desired outcome for the Transforming Technology project?

372. What is the difference between % Complete and % work?

373. What are the requirements for resource data?

374. How difficult will it be to do specific activities on this Transforming Technology project?

375. The list could probably go on, but, the thing that you would most like to know is, How long & How much?

2.17 Activity Duration Estimates: Transforming Technology

376. Are the causes of all variances identified?

377. What tasks must precede this task?

378. How does the job market and current state of the economy affect human resource management?

379. Does a process exist to identify Transforming Technology project roles, responsibilities and reporting relationships?

380. Who has the PRIMARY responsibility to solve this problem?

381. How does poking fun at technical professionals communications skills impact the industry and educational programs?

382. What are the main types of goods and services being outsourced?

383. Do procedures exist that identify when and how human resources are introduced and removed from the Transforming Technology project?

384. What type of activity sequencing method is required for corresponding activities?

385. Are adjustments implemented to correct or prevent defects?

386. Briefly summarize the work done by Maslow, Herzberg, McClellan, McGregor, Ouchi, Thamhain and Wilemon, and Covey. How do theories relate to Transforming Technology project management?

387. What functions does this software provide that cannot be done easily using other tools such as a spreadsheet or database?

388. How does Transforming Technology project integration management relate to the Transforming Technology project life cycle, stakeholders, and the other Transforming Technology project management knowledge areas?

389. Do stakeholders follow a procedure for formally accepting the Transforming Technology project scope?

390. Why is it difficult to use Transforming Technology project management software well?

391. Transforming Technology project manager has received activity duration estimates from his team. Which does one need in order to complete schedule development?

392. Is risk identification completed regularly throughout the Transforming Technology project?

393. How is the Transforming Technology project doing?

394. What are key inputs and outputs of the software?

2.18 Duration Estimating Worksheet: Transforming Technology

395. What is an Average Transforming Technology project?

396. Can the Transforming Technology project be constructed as planned?

397. When does your organization expect to be able to complete it?

398. Value pocket identification & quantification what are value pockets?

399. What questions do you have?

400. Define the work as completely as possible. What work will be included in the Transforming Technology project?

401. When, then?

402. What utility impacts are there?

403. Is a construction detail attached (to aid in explanation)?

404. Will the Transforming Technology project collaborate with the local community and leverage resources?

405. Does the Transforming Technology project

provide innovative ways for stakeholders to overcome obstacles or deliver better outcomes?

406. Is this operation cost effective?

407. Science = process: remember the scientific method?

408. How can the Transforming Technology project be displayed graphically to better visualize the activities?

409. Why estimate time and cost?

410. Do any colleagues have experience with your organization and/or RFPs?

411. Is the Transforming Technology project responsive to community need?

412. What are the critical bottleneck activities?

2.19 Project Schedule: Transforming Technology

413. Did the Transforming Technology project come in on schedule?

414. What is Transforming Technology project management?

415. Are you working on the right risks?

416. Meet requirements?

417. Schedule/cost recovery?

418. Did the final product meet or exceed user expectations?

419. What does that mean?

420. How do you use schedules?

421. To what degree is do you feel the entire team was committed to the Transforming Technology project schedule?

422. Have all Transforming Technology project delays been adequately accounted for, communicated to all stakeholders and adjustments made in overall Transforming Technology project schedule?

423. Is infrastructure setup part of your Transforming Technology project?

424. Are all remaining durations correct?

425. Why or why not?

426. How do you manage Transforming Technology project Risk?

427. Why do you think schedule issues often cause the most conflicts on Transforming Technology projects?

428. Eliminate unnecessary activities. Are there activities that came from a template or previous Transforming Technology project that are not applicable on this phase of this Transforming Technology project?

429. How do you know that youhave done this right?

430. Did the Transforming Technology project come in under budget?

2.20 Cost Management Plan: Transforming Technology

431. Were Transforming Technology project team members involved in the development of activity & task decomposition?

432. Are Transforming Technology project team members committed fulltime?

433. Is there anything unique in this Transforming Technology projects scope statement that will affect resources?

434. Is the schedule updated on a periodic basis?

435. The definition of the Transforming Technology project scope what needs to be accomplished?

436. Have activity relationships and interdependencies within tasks been adequately identified?

437. Does the Transforming Technology project have a formal Transforming Technology project Charter?

438. Scope of work – What is the likelihood and extent of potential future changes to the Transforming Technology project scope?

439. Who will prepare the cost estimates?

440. Has the business need been clearly defined?

441. Have the reasons why the changes to your organizational systems and capabilities are required?

442. Is an industry recognized mechanized support tool(s) being used for Transforming Technology project scheduling & tracking?

443. Estimating responsibilities – how will the responsibilities for cost estimating be allocated?

444. Are procurement deliverables arriving on time and to specification?

445. Have all team members been part of identifying risks?

446. Has a capability assessment been conducted?

447. If you sold 10x widgets on a day, what would the affect on costs be?

448. Is it a Transforming Technology project?

2.21 Activity Cost Estimates: Transforming Technology

449. Can you delete activities or make them inactive?

450. Review – what are some common errors in activities to avoid?

451. How do you allocate indirect costs to activities?

452. Padding is bad and contingencies are good. what is the difference?

453. How do you treat administrative costs in the activity inventory?

454. What is included in indirect cost being allocated?

455. What are you looking for?

456. Was it performed on time?

457. Can you change your activities?

458. How do you do activity recasts?

459. One way to define activities is to consider how organization employees describe jobs to families and friends. You basically want to know, What do you do?

460. What are the audit requirements?

461. Will you need to provide essential services

information about activities?

462. What makes a good expected result statement?

463. How many activities should you have?

464. What is the estimators estimating history?

465. Estimated cost?

466. Will you use any tools, such as Transforming Technology project management software, to assist in capturing Earned Value metrics?

2.22 Cost Estimating Worksheet: Transforming Technology

467. Is the Transforming Technology project responsive to community need?

468. What can be included?

469. What additional Transforming Technology project(s) could be initiated as a result of this Transforming Technology project?

470. Can a trend be established from historical performance data on the selected measure and are the criteria for using trend analysis or forecasting methods met?

471. What is the purpose of estimating?

472. Is it feasible to establish a control group arrangement?

473. What info is needed?

474. What happens to any remaining funds not used?

475. Who is best positioned to know and assist in identifying corresponding factors?

476. How will the results be shared and to whom?

477. What is the estimated labor cost today based upon this information?

478. Ask: are others positioned to know, are others credible, and will others cooperate?

479. Identify the timeframe necessary to monitor progress and collect data to determine how the selected measure has changed?

480. Does the Transforming Technology project provide innovative ways for stakeholders to overcome obstacles or deliver better outcomes?

481. Will the Transforming Technology project collaborate with the local community and leverage resources?

482. What costs are to be estimated?

483. What will others want?

2.23 Cost Baseline: Transforming Technology

484. What is cost and Transforming Technology project cost management?

485. Have the lessons learned been filed with the Transforming Technology project Management Office?

486. Does a process exist for establishing a cost baseline to measure Transforming Technology project performance?

487. Are there contingencies or conditions related to the acceptance?

488. How will cost estimates be used?

489. What is it ?

490. Impact to environment?

491. Are you meeting with your team regularly?

492. Why do you manage cost?

493. Escalation criteria met?

494. What would the life cycle costs be?

495. Will the Transforming Technology project fail if the change request is not executed?

496. On budget?

497. Does it impact schedule, cost, quality?

498. Have all the product or service deliverables been accepted by the customer?

499. Vac -variance at completion, how much over/ under budget do you expect to be?

500. At which frequency ?

501. Is the cr within Transforming Technology project scope?

502. Has the Transforming Technology projected annual cost to operate and maintain the product(s) or service(s) been approved and funded?

2.24 Quality Management Plan: Transforming Technology

503. How are changes recorded?

504. Have adequate resources been provided by management to ensure Transforming Technology project success?

505. Is a component/condition present?

506. How does your organization manage training and evaluate its effectiveness?

507. Are there trends or hot spots?

508. What are you trying to accomplish?

509. Sampling part of task?

510. What would be the next steps or what else should you do at this point?

511. Are decisions/actions based on data collected?

512. With the five whys method, the team considers why the issue being explored occurred. do others then take that initial answer and ask why?

513. How are deviations from procedures handled?

514. How does your organization establish and maintain customer relationships?

515. What is the return on investment?

516. Where do you focus?

517. Who gets results of work?

518. Does the Transforming Technology project have a formal Transforming Technology project Plan?

519. Who is responsible for approving the qapp?

520. Are you following the quality standards?

521. Is staff trained on the software technologies that are being used on the Transforming Technology project?

2.25 Quality Metrics: Transforming Technology

522. What metrics do you measure?

523. Are applicable standards referenced and available?

524. How do you calculate such metrics?

525. Can visual measures help you to filter visualizations of interest?

526. When will the Final Guidance will be issued?

527. Who notifies stakeholders of normal and abnormal results?

528. Do you stratify metrics by product or site?

529. Should a modifier be included?

530. The metrics–what is being considered?

531. What percentage are outcome-based?

532. Were quality attributes reported?

533. Where is quality now?

534. What makes a visualization memorable?

535. What group is empowered to define quality

requirements?

536. Is quality culture a competitive advantage?

537. What approved evidence based screening tools can be used?

538. How are requirements conflicts resolved?

539. How do you know if everyone is trying to improve the right things?

540. What happens if you get an abnormal result?

541. Does risk analysis documentation meet standards?

2.26 Process Improvement Plan: Transforming Technology

542. Have the supporting tools been developed or acquired?

543. Who should prepare the process improvement action plan?

544. What personnel are the sponsors for that initiative?

545. Management commitment at all levels?

546. What actions are needed to address the problems and achieve the goals?

547. What personnel are the change agents for your initiative?

548. Why do you want to achieve the goal?

549. What personnel are the champions for the initiative?

550. What is the test-cycle concept?

551. Where are you now?

552. What makes people good SPI coaches?

553. Are you making progress on the goals?

554. Everyone agrees on what process improvement is, right?

555. Does your process ensure quality?

556. The motive is determined by asking, Why do you want to achieve this goal?

557. Why quality management?

558. What lessons have you learned so far?

559. Where do you want to be?

2.27 Responsibility Assignment Matrix: Transforming Technology

560. How do you manage human resources?

561. What travel needed?

562. Are all authorized tasks assigned to identified organizational elements?

563. Who is responsible for work and budgets for each wbs?

564. Does the accounting system provide a basis for auditing records of direct costs chargeable to the contract?

565. Are too many reports done in writing instead of verbally?

566. Does the Transforming Technology project need to be analyzed further to uncover additional responsibilities?

567. Are there any drawbacks to using a responsibility assignment matrix?

568. What expertise is not available in your department?

569. Budgets assigned to major functional organizations?

570. What do people write/say on status/Transforming Technology project reports?

571. How many people do you need?

572. Is budgeted cost for work performed calculated in a manner consistent with the way work is planned?

573. The anticipated business volume?

574. Direct labor dollars and/or hours?

575. Are the bases and rates for allocating costs from each indirect pool consistently applied?

576. Budgeted cost for work scheduled?

577. Does a missing responsibility indicate that the current Transforming Technology project is not yet fully understood?

2.28 Roles and Responsibilities: Transforming Technology

578. Once the responsibilities are defined for the Transforming Technology project, have the deliverables, roles and responsibilities been clearly communicated to every participant?

579. Was the expectation clearly communicated?

580. What should you do now to ensure that you are exceeding expectations and excelling in your current position?

581. Are the quality assurance functions and related roles and responsibilities clearly defined?

582. Influence: what areas of organizational decision making are you able to influence when you do not have authority to make the final decision?

583. Do the values and practices inherent in the culture of your organization foster or hinder the process?

584. Is there a training program in place for stakeholders covering expectations, roles and responsibilities and any addition knowledge others need to be good stakeholders?

585. Required skills, knowledge, experience?

586. Are Transforming Technology project team roles

and responsibilities identified and documented?

587. Key conclusions and recommendations: Are conclusions and recommendations relevant and acceptable?

588. Is the data complete?

589. How is your work-life balance?

590. Concern: where are you limited or have no authority, where you can not influence?

591. Once the responsibilities are defined for the Transforming Technology project, have the deliverables, roles and responsibilities been clearly communicated to every participant?

592. What is working well?

593. Accountabilities: what are the roles and responsibilities of individual team members?

594. Who is responsible for each task?

595. Are governance roles and responsibilities documented?

596. Attainable / achievable: the goal is attainable; can you actually accomplish the goal?

597. Do you take the time to clearly define roles and responsibilities on Transforming Technology project tasks?

2.29 Human Resource Management Plan: Transforming Technology

598. Does the Transforming Technology project have a formal Transforming Technology project Charter?

599. What skills, knowledge and experiences are required?

600. Are quality inspections and review activities listed in the Transforming Technology project schedule(s)?

601. Are all key components of a Quality Assurance Plan present?

602. Are Transforming Technology project team roles and responsibilities identified and documented?

603. Is there an onboarding process in place?

604. Who are the people that make up your organization and whom create the success that your organization enjoys as a whole?

605. How will the Transforming Technology project manage expectations & meet needs and requirements?

606. What talent is needed?

607. Is your organization heading towards expansion, outsourcing of certain talents or making cut-backs to

save money?

608. Are all resource assumptions documented?

609. Who needs training?

610. Are quality metrics defined?

611. How relevant is this attribute to this Transforming Technology project or audit?

612. Is Transforming Technology project work proceeding in accordance with the original Transforming Technology project schedule?

2.30 Communications Management Plan: Transforming Technology

613. In your work, how much time is spent on stakeholder identification?

614. Who is involved as you identify stakeholders?

615. Timing: when do the effects of the communication take place?

616. What to know?

617. Who to share with?

618. What are the interrelationships?

619. What communications method?

620. How will the person responsible for executing the communication item be notified?

621. Will messages be directly related to the release strategy or phases of the Transforming Technology project?

622. What is the stakeholders level of authority?

623. What to learn?

624. How often do you engage with stakeholders?

625. Do you feel a register helps?

626. Are others needed?

627. Who did you turn to if you had questions?

628. Who were proponents/opponents?

629. What approaches do you use?

630. How much time does it take to do it?

631. Do you feel more overwhelmed by stakeholders?

2.31 Risk Management Plan: Transforming Technology

632. Are tools for analysis and design available?

633. Internal technical and management reviews?

634. Workarounds are determined during which step of risk management?

635. How are risk analvsis and prioritization performed?

636. Where are you confronted with risks during the business phases?

637. Is a software Transforming Technology project management tool available?

638. Is the process supported by tools?

639. Are people attending meetings and doing work?

640. Are tool mentors available?

641. Have customers been involved fully in the definition of requirements?

642. Was an original risk assessment/risk management plan completed?

643. Is the number of people on the Transforming Technology project team adequate to do the job?

644. Is this an issue, action item, question or a risk?

645. Is there additional information that would make you more confident about your analysis?

646. Is there anything you would now do differently on your Transforming Technology project based on this experience?

647. Number of users of the product?

648. What is the probability the risk avoidance strategy will be successful?

649. Have you worked with the customer in the past?

650. Are the reports useful and easy to read?

651. Which is an input to the risk management process?

2.32 Risk Register: Transforming Technology

652. Risk documentation: what reporting formats and processes will be used for risk management activities?

653. Have other controls and solutions been implemented in other services which could be applied as an alternative to additional funding?

654. User involvement: do you have the right users?

655. What is the reason for current performance gaps and do the risks and opportunities identified previously account for this?

656. Are corrective measures implemented as planned?

657. Budget and schedule: what are the estimated costs and schedules for performing risk-related activities?

658. Are your objectives at risk?

659. Who is going to do it?

660. When will it happen?

661. How could corresponding Risk affect the Transforming Technology project in terms of cost and schedule?

662. Are there any knock-on effects/impact on any of the other areas?

663. Are implemented controls working as others should?

664. What is a Risk?

665. Assume the event happens, what is the Most Likely impact?

666. Are there any gaps in the evidence?

667. Are there other alternative controls that could be implemented?

668. Who needs to know about this?

669. What should the audit role be in establishing a risk management process?

670. Which key risks have ineffective responses or outstanding improvement actions?

2.33 Probability and Impact Assessment: Transforming Technology

671. What is the likelihood?

672. Can this technology be absorbed with current level of expertise available in your organization?

673. Assuming that you have identified a number of risks in the Transforming Technology project, how would you prioritize them?

674. Is the customer willing to participate in reviews?

675. Do you have a mechanism for managing change?

676. My Transforming Technology project leader has suddenly left your organization, what do you do?

677. Do benefits and chances of success outweigh potential damage if success is not attained?

678. How would you suggest monitoring for risk transition indicators?

679. What are the tools and techniques used in managing the challenges faced?

680. What should be the requirement of organizational restructuring as each subTransforming Technology project goes through a different lifecycle phase?

681. When and how will the recent breakthroughs in basic research lead to commercial products?

682. Mitigation -how can you avoid the risk?

683. What are the current requirements of the customer?

684. Does the software engineering team have the right mix of skills?

685. Can you avoid altogether some things that might go wrong?

686. Can it be enlarged by drawing people from other areas of your organization?

687. How would you assess the risk management process in the Transforming Technology project?

688. What should be the level of coordination?

689. What would be the effect of slippage?

2.34 Probability and Impact Matrix: Transforming Technology

690. Are some people working on multiple Transforming Technology projects?

691. Are the risk data timely and relevant?

692. What will be the likely political situation during the life of the Transforming Technology project?

693. What risks were tracked?

694. What things might go wrong?

695. What should you do FIRST?

696. How do you define a risk?

697. What new technologies are being explored in the same area?

698. Is the number of people on the Transforming Technology project team adequate to do the job?

699. What is Transforming Technology project risk management?

700. What is the likelihood of a breakthrough?

701. Which risks need to move on to Perform Quantitative Risk Analysis?

702. Mandated delivery date?

703. What did not work so well?

704. What are the preparations required for facing difficulties?

705. During Transforming Technology project executing, a major problem occurs that was not included in the risk register. What should you do FIRST?

706. How are the local factors going to affect the absorption?

707. Are testing tools available and suitable?

708. Is Transforming Technology project scope stable?

709. Costs associated with late delivery or a defective product?

2.35 Risk Data Sheet: Transforming Technology

710. Will revised controls lead to tolerable risk levels?

711. During work activities could hazards exist?

712. What do people affected think about the need for, and practicality of preventive measures?

713. Type of risk identified?

714. What will be the consequences if the risk happens?

715. Potential for recurrence?

716. How can it happen?

717. Who has a vested interest in how you perform as your organization (our stakeholders)?

718. Is the data sufficiently specified in terms of the type of failure being analyzed, and its frequency or probability?

719. What is the environment within which you operate (social trends, economic, community values, broad based participation, national directions etc.)?

720. How reliable is the data source?

721. How can hazards be reduced?

722. What are you here for (Mission)?

723. Are new hazards created?

724. What is the chance that it will happen?

725. Do effective diagnostic tests exist?

726. What do you know?

727. What are the main opportunities available to you that you should grab while you can?

728. Whom do you serve (customers)?

2.36 Procurement Management Plan: Transforming Technology

729. Are corrective actions and variances reported?

730. Are Transforming Technology project team members committed fulltime?

731. Are risk triggers captured?

732. Have all involved Transforming Technology project stakeholders and work groups committed to the Transforming Technology project?

733. Are tasks tracked by hours?

734. What were things that you did very well and want to do the same again on the next Transforming Technology project?

735. Are decisions captured in a decisions log?

736. Is the communication plan being followed?

737. Have process improvement efforts been completed before requirements efforts begin?

738. Is there a procurement management plan in place?

739. Are updated Transforming Technology project time & resource estimates reasonable based on the current Transforming Technology project stage?

740. If standardized procurement documents are needed, where can others be found?

741. Is there a formal set of procedures supporting Issues Management?

742. Are the Transforming Technology project plans updated on a frequent basis?

2.37 Source Selection Criteria: Transforming Technology

743. What should a Draft Request for Proposal (DRFP) include?

744. What information is to be provided and when should it be provided?

745. What are the limitations on pre-competitive range communications?

746. Do you want to wait until all offerors have been evaluated?

747. What should be considered when developing evaluation standards?

748. How do you ensure an integrated assessment of proposals?

749. Are there any specific considerations that precludes offers from being selected as the awardee?

750. Do you prepare an independent cost estimate?

751. Can you reasonably estimate total organization requirements for the coming year?

752. What is cost analysis and when should it be performed?

753. What aspects should the contracting officer

brief the Transforming Technology project on prior to evaluation of proposals?

754. If the costs are normalized, please account for how the normalization is conducted. Is a cost realism analysis used?

755. Will the technical evaluation factor unnecessarily force the acquisition into a higher-priced market segment?

756. What should clarifications include?

757. Are evaluators ready to begin this task?

758. Who should attend debriefings?

759. What are the steps in performing a cost/tech tradeoff?

760. What should preproposal conferences accomplish?

761. What should be considered?

762. How do you facilitate evaluation against published criteria?

2.38 Stakeholder Management Plan: Transforming Technology

763. Are action items captured and managed?

764. If a problem has been detected, what tools can be used to determine a root cause?

765. Is the Transforming Technology project sponsor clearly communicating the business case or rationale for why this Transforming Technology project is needed?

766. Is quality monitored from the perspective of the customers needs and expectations?

767. Are changes in scope (deliverable commitments) agreed to by all affected groups & individuals?

768. Have all stakeholders been identified?

769. Have key stakeholders been identified?

770. Is there a formal process for updating the Transforming Technology project baseline?

771. Why would you develop a Transforming Technology project Business Plan?

772. Have stakeholder accountabilities & responsibilities been clearly defined?

773. Is there an issues management plan in place?

774. Is stakeholder involvement adequate?

775. Are best practices and metrics employed to identify issues, progress, performance, etc.?

776. What records are required (eg purchase orders, agreements)?

2.39 Change Management Plan: Transforming Technology

777. Where will the funds come from?

778. What prerequisite knowledge or training is required?

779. Who will fund the training?

780. What are the major changes to processes?

781. What roles within your organization are affected, and how?

782. Are there any restrictions on who can receive the communications?

783. What tasks are needed?

784. What new roles are needed?

785. Who will be the change levers?

786. Have the business unit contacts been briefed by the Transforming Technology project team?

787. Who might present the most resistance?

788. Change invariability confront many relationships especially the already stated that require a set of behaviours What roles with in your organization are affected and how?

789. How much change management is needed?

790. Will the culture embrace or reject this change?

791. Is there a support model for this application and are the details available for distribution?

792. Are there resource implications for your communications strategy?

793. Why is it important?

794. What does a resilient organization look like?

795. What are the responsibilities assigned to each role?

796. What is the worst thing that can happen if you chose not to communicate this information?

3.0 Executing Process Group: Transforming Technology

797. What were things that you did very well and want to do the same again on the next Transforming Technology project?

798. What will you do to minimize the impact should a risk event occur?

799. How well defined and documented were the Transforming Technology project management processes you chose to use?

800. Contingency planning. if a risk event occurs, what will you do?

801. How do you prevent staff are just doing busywork to pass the time?

802. Are decisions made in a timely manner?

803. Does the Transforming Technology project team have the right skills?

804. When is the appropriate time to bring the scorecard to Board meetings?

805. How can software assist in procuring goods and services?

806. Is the Transforming Technology project performing better or worse than planned?

807. What are the critical steps involved with strategy mapping?

808. Is the Transforming Technology project making progress in helping to achieve the set results?

809. Is activity definition the first process involved in Transforming Technology project time management?

810. Will outside resources be needed to help?

811. After how many days will the lease cost be the same as the purchase cost for the equipment?

812. How will professionals learn what is expected from them what the deliverables are?

813. What are the main types of contracts if you do decide to outsource?

814. Does the case present a realistic scenario?

3.1 Team Member Status Report: Transforming Technology

815. Do you have an Enterprise Transforming Technology project Management Office (EPMO)?

816. What is to be done?

817. How can you make it practical?

818. Does the product, good, or service already exist within your organization?

819. Does every department have to have a Transforming Technology project Manager on staff?

820. Are the products of your organizations Transforming Technology projects meeting customers objectives?

821. Is there evidence that staff is taking a more professional approach toward management of your organizations Transforming Technology projects?

822. When a teams productivity and success depend on collaboration and the efficient flow of information, what generally fails them?

823. Will the staff do training or is that done by a third party?

824. How much risk is involved?

825. Does your organization have the means (staff, money, contract, etc.) to produce or to acquire the product, good, or service?

826. What specific interest groups do you have in place?

827. Why is it to be done?

828. Are your organizations Transforming Technology projects more successful over time?

829. The problem with Reward & Recognition Programs is that the truly deserving people all too often get left out. How can you make it practical?

830. How will resource planning be done?

831. Are the attitudes of staff regarding Transforming Technology project work improving?

832. How it is to be done?

833. How does this product, good, or service meet the needs of the Transforming Technology project and your organization as a whole?

3.2 Change Request: Transforming Technology

834. What is the relationship between requirements attributes and reliability?

835. What can be filed?

836. Have scm procedures for noting the change, recording it, and reporting it been followed?

837. How is quality being addressed on the Transforming Technology project?

838. Describe how modifications, enhancements, defects and/or deficiencies shall be notified (e.g. Problem Reports, Change Requests etc) and managed. Detail warranty and/or maintenance periods?

839. Where do changes come from?

840. When do you create a change request?

841. Who is responsible to authorize changes?

842. What is the relationship between requirements attributes and attributes like complexity and size?

843. Why were your requested changes rejected or not made?

844. Has a formal technical review been conducted to

assess technical correctness?

845. What are the Impacts to your organization?

846. What is the change request log?

847. Will all change requests and current status be logged?

848. Can static requirements change attributes like the size of the change be used to predict reliability in execution?

849. Who is included in the change control team?

850. How can you ensure that changes have been made properly?

851. Have all related configuration items been properly updated?

852. Who can suggest changes?

3.3 Change Log: Transforming Technology

853. How does this change affect scope?

854. When was the request approved?

855. Is this a mandatory replacement?

856. Does the suggested change request represent a desired enhancement to the products functionality?

857. Is the change request within Transforming Technology project scope?

858. Will the Transforming Technology project fail if the change request is not executed?

859. How does this relate to the standards developed for specific business processes?

860. Do the described changes impact on the integrity or security of the system?

861. Who initiated the change request?

862. Is the change request open, closed or pending?

863. Should a more thorough impact analysis be conducted?

864. Is the submitted change a new change or a modification of a previously approved change?

865. How does this change affect the timeline of the schedule?

866. When was the request submitted?

867. Is the change backward compatible without limitations?

868. Is the requested change request a result of changes in other Transforming Technology project(s)?

869. Does the suggested change request seem to represent a necessary enhancement to the product?

3.4 Decision Log: Transforming Technology

870. What is the average size of your matters in an applicable measurement?

871. What is your overall strategy for quality control / quality assurance procedures?

872. Linked to original objective?

873. Decision-making process; how will the team make decisions?

874. It becomes critical to track and periodically revisit both operational effectiveness; Are you noticing all that you need to, and are you interpreting what you see effectively?

875. Meeting purpose; why does this team meet?

876. How does an increasing emphasis on cost containment influence the strategies and tactics used?

877. At what point in time does loss become unacceptable?

878. Which variables make a critical difference?

879. What makes you different or better than others companies selling the same thing?

880. Is your opponent open to a non-traditional workflow, or will it likely challenge anything you do?

881. How effective is maintaining the log at facilitating organizational learning?

882. Who will be given a copy of this document and where will it be kept?

883. What are the cost implications?

884. Adversarial environment. is your opponent open to a non-traditional workflow, or will it likely challenge anything you do?

885. How does provision of information, both in terms of content and presentation, influence acceptance of alternative strategies?

886. How does the use a Decision Support System influence the strategies/tactics or costs?

887. What was the rationale for the decision?

888. Who is the decisionmaker?

889. Is everything working as expected?

3.5 Quality Audit: Transforming Technology

890. How does your organization know that its range of activities are being reviewed as rigorously and constructively as they could be?

891. Is there a written corporate quality policy?

892. Are people allowed to contribute ideas?

893. How does your organization know that its relationships with the community at large are appropriately effective and constructive?

894. Is the process of self review, learning and improvement endemic throughout your organization?

895. How does the organization know that its system for maintaining and advancing the capabilities of its staff, particularly in relation to the Mission of the organization, is appropriately effective and constructive?

896. Are measuring and test equipment that have been placed out of service suitably identified and excluded from use in any device reconditioning operation?

897. Are all complaints involving the possible failure of a device, labeling, or packaging to meet any of its specifications reviewed, evaluated, and investigated?

898. Are salvageable and salvaged medical devices stored in a manner to prevent damage and/or contamination?

899. How do you know what, specifically, is required of you in your work?

900. How does your organization know that its relationships with other relevant organizations are appropriately effective and constructive?

901. How does your organization know that the range and quality of its accommodation, catering and transportation services are appropriately effective and constructive?

902. How does your organization know that its system for examining work done is appropriately effective and constructive?

903. How does your organization know that the review processes are effective?

904. What has changed/improved as a result of the review processes?

905. Are there appropriate means for intervening if necessary?

906. How does your organization know that its security arrangements are appropriately effective and constructive?

907. Do the acceptance procedures and specifications include the criteria for acceptance/rejection, define

the process to be used, and specify the measuring and test equipment that is to be used?

908. How does your organization know that its management of its ethical responsibilities is appropriately effective and constructive?

909. How does your organization know that the range and quality of its social and recreational services and facilities are appropriately effective and constructive in meeting the needs of staff?

3.6 Team Directory: Transforming Technology

910. Where should the information be distributed?

911. Process decisions: do job conditions warrant additional actions to collect job information and document on-site activity?

912. Decisions: is the most suitable form of contract being used?

913. Process decisions: is work progressing on schedule and per contract requirements?

914. What needs to be communicated?

915. Who will report Transforming Technology project status to all stakeholders?

916. When does information need to be distributed?

917. Is construction on schedule?

918. Process decisions: are contractors adequately prosecuting the work?

919. Days from the time the issue is identified?

920. Where will the product be used and/or delivered or built when appropriate?

921. How does the team resolve conflicts and ensure

tasks are completed?

922. When will you produce deliverables?

923. Decisions: what could be done better to improve the quality of the constructed product?

924. How and in what format should information be presented?

925. Process decisions: do invoice amounts match accepted work in place?

926. Process decisions: how well was task order work performed?

927. Who will talk to the customer?

928. Who are the Team Members?

3.7 Team Operating Agreement: Transforming Technology

929. Did you recap the meeting purpose, time, and expectations?

930. What is culture?

931. Why does your organization want to participate in teaming?

932. Resource allocation: how will individual team members account for time and expenses, and how will this be allocated in the team budget?

933. How do you want to be thought of and known within your organization?

934. Do you upload presentation materials in advance and test the technology?

935. Reimbursements: how will the team members be reimbursed for expenses and time commitments?

936. What are the boundaries (organizational or geographic) within which you operate?

937. How will you resolve conflict efficiently and respectfully?

938. How will you divide work equitably?

939. To whom do you deliver your services?

940. Are there more than two functional areas represented by your team?

941. What is your unique contribution to your organization?

942. Do you use a parking lot for any items that are important and outside of the agenda?

943. Are leadership responsibilities shared among team members (versus a single leader)?

944. What are the safety issues/risks that need to be addressed and/or that the team needs to consider?

945. Do you call or email participants to ensure understanding, follow-through and commitment to the meeting outcomes?

946. Do team members need to frequently communicate as a full group to make timely decisions?

947. Are there influences outside the team that may affect performance, and if so, have you identified and addressed them?

3.8 Team Performance Assessment: Transforming Technology

948. How do you keep key people outside the group informed about its accomplishments?

949. Lack of method variance in self-reported affect and perceptions at work: Reality or artifact?

950. How much interpersonal friction is there in your team?

951. To what degree do members understand and articulate the same purpose without relying on ambiguous abstractions?

952. To what degree are the goals realistic?

953. To what degree does the teams purpose contain themes that are particularly meaningful and memorable?

954. Do you promptly inform members about major developments that may affect them?

955. To what degree will the team adopt a concrete, clearly understood, and agreed-upon approach that will result in achievement of the teams goals?

956. To what degree does the teams work approach provide opportunity for members to engage in open interaction?

957. What structural changes have you made or are you preparing to make?

958. To what degree are the skill areas critical to team performance present?

959. To what degree does the teams work approach provide opportunity for members to engage in fact-based problem solving?

960. To what degree is the team cognizant of small wins to be celebrated along the way?

961. To what degree are staff involved as partners in the improvement process?

962. To what degree are fresh input and perspectives systematically caught and added (for example, through information and analysis, new members, and senior sponsors)?

963. Effects of crew composition on crew performance: Does the whole equal the sum of its parts?

964. Does more radicalness mean more perceived benefits?

965. To what degree are corresponding categories of skills either actually or potentially represented across the membership?

966. To what degree will team members, individually and collectively, commit time to help themselves and others learn and develop skills?

967. Where to from here?

3.9 Team Member Performance Assessment: Transforming Technology

968. How often are assessments to be conducted?

969. What were the challenges that resulted for training and assessment?

970. Did training work?

971. What is a significant fact or event?

972. What makes them effective?

973. What entity leads the process, selects a potential restructuring option and develops the plan?

974. How do you work together to improve teaching and learning?

975. Does the rater (supervisor) have to wait for the interim or final performance assessment review to tell an employee that the employees performance is unsatisfactory?

976. To what degree do the goals specify concrete team work products?

977. New skills/knowledge gained this year?

978. What are best practices for delivering and developing training evaluations to maximize the

benefits of leveraging emerging technologies?

979. Are the goals SMART ?

980. How is the timing of assessments organized (e.g., pre/post-test, single point during training, multiple reassessment during training)?

981. What are the evaluation strategies (e.g., reaction, learning, behavior, results) used. What evaluation results did you have?

982. Are there any safeguards to prevent intentional or unintentional rating errors?

983. Are the draft goals SMART ?

984. Who receives a benchmark visit?

985. To what degree does the team possess adequate membership to achieve its ends?

3.10 Issue Log: Transforming Technology

986. Is the issue log kept in a safe place?

987. What help do you and your team need from the stakeholders?

988. Is access to the Issue Log controlled?

989. How were past initiatives successful?

990. Why do you manage communications?

991. What are the stakeholders interrelationships?

992. Are they needed?

993. Is it a change in scope?

994. What would have to change?

995. Which stakeholders can influence others?

996. Who are the members of the governing body?

997. What date was the issue resolved?

998. Do you often overlook a key stakeholder or stakeholder group?

999. Who do you turn to if you have questions?

1000. Do you have members of your team responsible for certain stakeholders?

4.0 Monitoring and Controlling Process Group: Transforming Technology

1001. Purpose: toward what end is the evaluation being conducted?

1002. Do the products created live up to the necessary quality?

1003. How were collaborations developed, and how are they sustained?

1004. What areas does the group agree are the biggest success on the Transforming Technology project?

1005. Use: how will they use the information?

1006. Measurable - are the targets measurable?

1007. Just how important is your work to the overall success of the Transforming Technology project?

1008. What areas were overlooked on this Transforming Technology project?

1009. Where is the Risk in the Transforming Technology project?

1010. Did the Transforming Technology project team have the right skills?

1011. Have operating capacities been created and/or reinforced in partners?

1012. What do they need to know about the Transforming Technology project?

1013. How are you doing?

1014. What resources are necessary?

1015. How well did the team follow the chosen processes?

1016. Does the solution fit in with organizations technical architectural requirements?

1017. What are the goals of the program?

1018. Is there sufficient time allotted between the general system design and the detailed system design phases?

4.1 Project Performance Report: Transforming Technology

1019. To what degree are the tasks requirements reflected in the flow and storage of information?

1020. To what degree does the task meet individual needs?

1021. To what degree do all members feel responsible for all agreed-upon measures?

1022. To what degree are the members clear on what they are individually responsible for and what they are jointly responsible for?

1023. To what degree will the team ensure that all members equitably share the work essential to the success of the team?

1024. To what degree do team members feel that the purpose of the team is important, if not exciting?

1025. What is the degree to which rules govern information exchange between individuals within your organization?

1026. To what degree does the funding match the requirement?

1027. What degree are the relative importance and priority of the goals clear to all team members?

1028. To what degree is there centralized control of information sharing?

1029. To what degree are the teams goals and objectives clear, simple, and measurable?

1030. To what degree can the team measure progress against specific goals?

1031. To what degree can all members engage in open and interactive considerations?

1032. To what degree do individual skills and abilities match task demands?

1033. How will procurement be coordinated with other Transforming Technology project aspects, such as scheduling and performance reporting?

1034. To what degree are the demands of the task compatible with and converge with the mission and functions of the formal organization?

1035. To what degree do team members agree with the goals, relative importance, and the ways in which achievement will be measured?

1036. What is the PRS?

4.2 Variance Analysis: Transforming Technology

1037. What does an unfavorable overhead volume variance mean?

1038. Are there knowledgeable Transforming Technology projections of future performance?

1039. Why do variances exist?

1040. Are significant decision points, constraints, and interfaces identified as key milestones?

1041. How are variances affected by multiple material and labor categories?

1042. There are detailed schedules which support control account and work package start and completion dates/events?

1043. What is the incurrence of actual indirect costs in excess of budgets, by element of expense?

1044. What business event caused the fluctuation?

1045. Contract line items and end items?

1046. Are material costs reported within the same period as that in which BCWP is earned for that material?

1047. Is work progressively subdivided into detailed

work packages as requirements are defined?

1048. Are records maintained to show how undistributed budgets are controlled?

1049. Is the market likely to continue to grow at this rate next year?

1050. What should management do?

1051. Did an existing competitor change strategy?

1052. How does your organization measure performance?

1053. Other relevant issues of Variance Analysis -selling price or gross margin?

1054. Did a new competitor enter the market?

1055. Is there a logical explanation for any variance?

4.3 Earned Value Status: Transforming Technology

1056. How much is it going to cost by the finish?

1057. If earned value management (EVM) is so good in determining the true status of a Transforming Technology project and Transforming Technology project its completion, why is it that hardly any one uses it in information systems related Transforming Technology projects?

1058. When is it going to finish?

1059. Where is evidence-based earned value in your organization reported?

1060. Earned value can be used in almost any Transforming Technology project situation and in almost any Transforming Technology project environment. it may be used on large Transforming Technology projects, medium sized Transforming Technology projects, tiny Transforming Technology projects (in cut-down form), complex and simple Transforming Technology projects and in any market sector. some people, of course, know all about earned value, they have used it for years - but perhaps not as effectively as they could have?

1061. What is the unit of forecast value?

1062. Where are your problem areas?

1063. Verification is a process of ensuring that the developed system satisfies the stakeholders agreements and specifications; Are you building the product right? What do you verify?

1064. How does this compare with other Transforming Technology projects?

1065. Validation is a process of ensuring that the developed system will actually achieve the stakeholders desired outcomes; Are you building the right product? What do you validate?

1066. Are you hitting your Transforming Technology projects targets?

4.4 Risk Audit: Transforming Technology

1067. Have permissions or required permits to use facilities managed by other parties been obtained?

1068. Does your organization meet the terms of any contracts with which it is involved?

1069. Do you conduct risk assessments on all programs, activities and events?

1070. Is your organization willing to commit significant time to the requirements gathering process?

1071. Do you have position descriptions for all key paid and volunteer positions in your organization?

1072. Are all programs planned and conducted according to recognized safety standards?

1073. Are end-users enthusiastically committed to the Transforming Technology project and the system/product to be built?

1074. To what extent are auditors influenced by the business risk assessment in the audit process, and how can auditors create more effective mental models to more fully examine contradictory evidence?

1075. Do requirements put excessive performance

constraints on the product?

1076. To what extent should analytical procedures be utilized in the risk-assessment process?

1077. What does monitoring consist of?

1078. Are you meeting your legal, regulatory and compliance requirements - if not, why not?

1079. Is the technology to be built new to your organization?

1080. Have all involved been advised of any obligations they have to sponsors?

1081. Is the number of people on the Transforming Technology project team adequate to do the job?

1082. Have you reviewed your constitution within the last twelve months?

1083. Is Transforming Technology project scope stable?

1084. What can be measured?

4.5 Contractor Status Report: Transforming Technology

1085. What was the final actual cost?

1086. What are the minimum and optimal bandwidth requirements for the proposed solution?

1087. How does the proposed individual meet each requirement?

1088. If applicable; describe your standard schedule for new software version releases. Are new software version releases included in the standard maintenance plan?

1089. What was the actual budget or estimated cost for your organizations services?

1090. What is the average response time for answering a support call?

1091. Describe how often regular updates are made to the proposed solution. Are corresponding regular updates included in the standard maintenance plan?

1092. Who can list a Transforming Technology project as organization experience, your organization or a previous employee of your organization?

1093. What process manages the contracts?

1094. Are there contractual transfer concerns?

1095. What was the budget or estimated cost for your organizations services?

1096. What was the overall budget or estimated cost?

1097. How is risk transferred?

1098. How long have you been using the services?

4.6 Formal Acceptance: Transforming Technology

1099. Was the client satisfied with the Transforming Technology project results?

1100. What was done right?

1101. What features, practices, and processes proved to be strengths or weaknesses?

1102. Do you buy pre-configured systems or build your own configuration?

1103. How well did the team follow the methodology?

1104. Was the Transforming Technology project goal achieved?

1105. Does it do what Transforming Technology project team said it would?

1106. How does your team plan to obtain formal acceptance on your Transforming Technology project?

1107. Did the Transforming Technology project manager and team act in a professional and ethical manner?

1108. Who supplies data?

1109. What can you do better next time?

1110. Was the sponsor/customer satisfied?

1111. What lessons were learned about your Transforming Technology project management methodology?

1112. Do you buy-in installation services?

1113. Was the Transforming Technology project work done on time, within budget, and according to specification?

1114. General estimate of the costs and times to complete the Transforming Technology project?

1115. Was business value realized?

1116. Do you perform formal acceptance or burn-in tests?

1117. What are the requirements against which to test, Who will execute?

1118. What is the Acceptance Management Process?

5.0 Closing Process Group: Transforming Technology

1119. What is the Transforming Technology project name and date of completion?

1120. Is the Transforming Technology project funded?

1121. Were sponsors and decision makers available when needed outside regularly scheduled meetings?

1122. What communication items need improvement?

1123. Mitigate. what will you do to minimize the impact should a risk event occur?

1124. Did the Transforming Technology project team have enough people to execute the Transforming Technology project plan?

1125. Was the user/client satisfied with the end product?

1126. What could be done to improve the process?

1127. What were the actual outcomes?

1128. Is this a follow-on to a previous Transforming Technology project?

1129. What is the overall risk of the Transforming Technology project to your organization?

1130. Can the lesson learned be replicated?

1131. Were the outcomes different from the already stated planned?

1132. Just how important is your work to the overall success of the Transforming Technology project?

1133. Is this a follow-on to a previous Transforming Technology project?

1134. What is the amount of funding and what Transforming Technology project phases are funded?

1135. What areas were overlooked on this Transforming Technology project?

1136. How will staff learn how to use the deliverables?

5.1 Procurement Audit: Transforming Technology

1137. Does the procurement function/unit have the ability to negotiate with customers and suppliers?

1138. Are controls proportionated to risks?

1139. Does your organization maintain a current file of vendors and vendor catalogues?

1140. Is the purchasing department consulted on favorable purchasing opportunities, economic ordering quantities, and revision of purchasing specifications?

1141. Is there a procedure to summarize bids and select a vendor?

1142. Was the estimated contract value in line with the final cost of the contract awarded?

1143. Are buyers rotated so that they do not deal with the same vendors year in and year out?

1144. Are required quality and service standards set?

1145. Are the right skills, experiences and competencies present in the acquisition workgroup and are the necessary outside specialists involved in part of the process?

1146. Is funding made available for payments

under the contract at the appropriate time and in accordance with the relevant national/public financial procedures?

1147. Are the responsibilities of the purchasing department clearly defined?

1148. When tenders were actually rejected because they were abnormally low, were reasons for this decision given and were they sufficiently grounded?

1149. Was a formal review of tenders received undertaken?

1150. Are the rules for automatic payment in computer programs approved by management prior to implementation?

1151. Are information gathered to produce knowledge about procured goods and services, prices paid and supplier performance?

1152. Are there mechanisms in place to evaluate the performance of the departments suppliers?

1153. Are there mechanisms for evaluating the departments suppliers performance in relation to prices, quality, delivery and innovation?

1154. Are purchase orders pre-numbered?

1155. Is there a system in place to handle partial delivery of orders, back orders, and partial payments?

1156. Are advance payments to employees properly authorized and controlled?

5.2 Contract Close-Out: Transforming Technology

1157. Was the contract complete without requiring numerous changes and revisions?

1158. Parties: Authorized?

1159. What happens to the recipient of services?

1160. Have all contracts been completed?

1161. Was the contract type appropriate?

1162. Have all contracts been closed?

1163. How is the contracting office notified of the automatic contract close-out?

1164. Have all contract records been included in the Transforming Technology project archives?

1165. How does it work?

1166. Has each contract been audited to verify acceptance and delivery?

1167. Parties: who is involved?

1168. Are the signers the authorized officials?

1169. Have all acceptance criteria been met prior to final payment to contractors?

1170. Was the contract sufficiently clear so as not to result in numerous disputes and misunderstandings?

1171. Change in circumstances?

1172. Change in knowledge?

1173. What is capture management?

1174. Change in attitude or behavior?

1175. How/when used ?

5.3 Project or Phase Close-Out: Transforming Technology

1176. Planned completion date?

1177. In preparing the Lessons Learned report, should it reflect a consensus viewpoint, or should the report reflect the different individual viewpoints?

1178. In addition to assessing whether the Transforming Technology project was successful, it is equally critical to analyze why it was or was not fully successful. Are you including this?

1179. Who controlled the resources for the Transforming Technology project?

1180. Who controlled key decisions that were made?

1181. What was learned?

1182. What were the goals and objectives of the communications strategy for the Transforming Technology project?

1183. Who are the Transforming Technology project stakeholders and what are roles and involvement?

1184. How often did each stakeholder need an update?

1185. What are they?

1186. How much influence did the stakeholder have over others?

1187. Were messages directly related to the release strategy or phases of the Transforming Technology project?

1188. Is the lesson significant, valid, and applicable?

1189. What benefits or impacts does the stakeholder group expect to obtain as a result of the Transforming Technology project?

1190. When and how were information needs best met?

1191. Have business partners been involved extensively, and what data was required for them?

1192. What could have been improved?

1193. Complete yes or no?

5.4 Lessons Learned: Transforming Technology

1194. How comprehensive was integration testing?

1195. How effective were your functional specs?

1196. What were the major enablers to a quick response?

1197. How well prepared were you to receive Transforming Technology project deliverables?

1198. If you had to do this Transforming Technology project again, what is the one thing that you would change (related to process, not to technical solutions)?

1199. What are the expectations of the individuals?

1200. Are lessons learned documented?

1201. How to write up the lesson identified – how will you document the results of your analysis corresponding that you have an li ready to take the next step in the ll process?

1202. What would you change?

1203. What mistakes did you successfully avoid making?

1204. Is there a clear cause and effect between the

activity and the lesson learned?

1205. Do you conduct the engineering tests?

1206. What were the main bottlenecks on the process?

1207. How much communication is task-related?

1208. What are the needs of the individuals?

1209. Are new goals needed?

1210. How clear were you on your role in the Transforming Technology project?

1211. Are you in full regulatory compliance?

1212. How complete and timely were the materials you were provided to decide whether to proceed from one Transforming Technology project lifecycle phase to the next?

Index

allows 11, 174
almost 255
already   127, 223, 227, 264
altogether   212
always 11
Amazon   12
ambiguous   242
amount   20, 160, 166, 264
amounts   239
amplify73, 124
analvsis   207
analysis   3, 6, 13, 50, 53-54, 56, 59-63, 66, 75, 77, 80-81, 86,
91, 96, 144, 153, 178, 189, 196, 207-208, 213, 219-220, 231, 243,
253-254, 271
analytical   258
analytics   49, 53
analyze   2, 48, 60, 64-65, 68-70, 85, 167, 269
analyzed   52, 57, 59, 62-64, 94, 109, 153, 158, 165, 199, 215
annual 192
another   12, 162
answer 13-14, 18, 30, 47, 68, 84, 101, 113, 159, 193
answered   29, 46, 66, 82, 100, 112, 136
answering   13, 259
anticipate   159
anybody   146
anyone   33, 122, 130, 144
anything   170, 176, 185, 208, 234
appear   1
applicable   14, 104, 184, 195, 233, 259, 270
applied   171, 200, 209
appointed   32, 36
approach   57, 92, 123, 132, 166, 227, 242-243
approaches   88, 93, 206
approval   40, 114
approvals   161
approved   31, 75, 156, 192, 196, 231, 266
approving   156, 194
Architects   8
archives   267
around114, 122
arriving186
articulate   242
artifact242

275

problems   20, 22-23, 25, 27-28, 53, 86, 99, 110, 129, 145, 154, 158, 197
procedure   180, 265
procedures   12, 104-105, 108, 110, 150, 165-166, 176, 179, 193, 218, 229, 233, 236, 258, 266
proceed   272
proceeding   204
process   1-6, 8, 12, 31, 35-37, 39, 42, 45, 49, 51, 55, 57, 60-62, 68-69, 71-75, 77-78, 80-82, 91-92, 96-97, 101-102, 104-106, 108, 111, 139, 141, 146-147, 150, 152-156, 158-161, 164, 176, 179, 182, 191, 197-198, 201, 203, 207-208, 210, 212, 217, 221, 225-226, 233, 235, 237-239, 243, 245, 249, 256-259, 262-263, 265, 271-272
processes   31, 54, 57, 66, 70, 72-75, 79-80, 82, 108-109, 147, 150, 160, 209, 223, 225, 231, 236, 250, 261
procured   266
procuring   225
produce   77, 147, 176, 228, 239, 266
produced   72, 88
produces   170
producing   156
product   1, 12, 58, 78, 80, 132, 136, 152, 172, 183, 192, 195, 208, 214, 227-228, 232, 238-239, 256-258, 263
production   44, 86, 129, 144, 160
products   1, 19, 25, 65, 115, 120, 141, 146, 156, 212, 227, 231, 245, 249
program   28, 56, 104, 146, 201, 250
programs   147, 179, 228, 257, 266
progress   37, 60, 100, 102, 123, 131, 190, 197, 222, 226, 252
project 2-4, 6-8, 10, 19, 23, 25, 28, 30, 72-73, 80, 104-105, 108, 114, 117, 121-122, 128-129, 131, 133, 135-136, 138-153, 156, 158-163, 166-170, 172, 174-175, 177-186, 188-194, 199-205, 207-209, 211-214, 217-218, 220-221, 223, 225-229, 231-232, 238, 249-252, 255, 257-259, 261-264, 267, 269-272
projected   164-165, 192
projection   166
projects   2, 119, 123, 138, 147, 156, 158, 163, 184-185, 213, 227-228, 255-256
promising   132
promote   65, 78
promptly   139, 242
proofing   97
proper 107, 164
properly   12, 43-44, 63, 230, 266

303

CPSIA information can be obtained
at www.ICGtesting.com
Printed in the USA
BVHW041216110719
553191BV00015B/1077/P